▶ Bending the Arc of Innovation

DOI: 10.1057/9781137370884

*Science, Technology, and Innovation Policy*

Series Editor: **Albert N. Link**
Managing Editor: **Charlotte Maiorana**

*Science, Technology, and Innovation Policy* is a scholarly series for academics and policy makers. Topics of interest include, but are not limited to, the economic foundations of science, technology, and innovation policy; the impact of science, technology, and innovation policy on economic growth and development; science, technology, and innovation policy as a driver of sustainability and social well-bring; and the application of methods and models for quantifying the social consequences of science, technology, and innovation policy.

*Titles include:*

*Congress's Own Think Tank: Learning from the Legacy of the Office of Technology Assessment (1972–1995)*
Peter D. Blair
*National Research Council*

*Bending the Arc of Innovation: Public Support of R&D in Small, Entrepreneurial Firms*
Albert N. Link
*University of North Carolina at Greensboro*
John T. Scott
*Dartmouth College*

DOI: 10.1057/9781137370884

palgrave▶pivot

# Bending the Arc of Innovation: Public Support of R&D in Small, Entrepreneurial Firms

Albert N. Link
*Professor of Economics, University of North Carolina at Greensboro*

and

John T. Scott
*Professor of Economics, Dartmouth College*

DOI: 10.1057/9781137370884

First published in 2013 by
PALGRAVE MACMILLAN®
in the United States—a division of St. Martin's Press LLC,
175 Fifth Avenue, New York, NY 10010.

Where this book is distributed in the UK, Europe and the rest of the world,
this is by Palgrave Macmillan, a division of Macmillan Publishers Limited,
registered in England, company number 785998, of Houndmills,
Basingstoke, Hampshire RG21 6XS.

Palgrave Macmillan is the global academic imprint of the above companies
and has companies and representatives throughout the world.

Palgrave® and Macmillan® are registered trademarks in the United States,
the United Kingdom, Europe and other countries.

ISBN: 978–1–137–37097–6  EPUB
ISBN: 978–1–137–37088–4  PDF
ISBN: 978–1–137–37158–4  Hardback

Library of Congress Cataloging-in-Publication Data is available from the
Library of Congress.

A catalogue record of the book is available from the British Library.

First edition: 2013

www.palgrave.com/pivot

DOI: 10.1057/9781137370884

# Contents

DOI: 10.1057/9781137370884

# List of Tables

DOI: 10.1057/9781137370884

# List of Figures

# About the Authors

**Albert N. Link** is Professor of Economics at the University of North Carolina at Greensboro (UNCG). He received the B.S. in Mathematics from the University of Richmond and the Ph.D. in Economics from Tulane University. After receiving the Ph.D., he joined the economics faculty at Auburn University where he remained until 1982 when he joined the economics faculty at UNCG. While at UNCG he has served as Head of the Department of Economics as well as Director of the M.B.A. program.

Professor Link's research focuses on innovation policy, academic entrepreneurship, and the economics of R&D. He is the Editor-in-Chief of the *Journal of Technology Transfer*. Among his most recent books with John Scott are *Employment Growth from Public Support of Innovation in Small Firms* (W.E. Upjohn Institute for Employment Research, 2012), *The Economics of Evaluation in Public Programs* (2011), and *Public Goods, Public Gains: Calculating the Social Benefits of Public R&D* (2011). Other recent books by Professor Link include *Handbook on the Theory and Practice of Program Evaluation* (2013), *Public Investments in Energy Technology* (2012), and *Government as Entrepreneur* (2009). His other research has appeared in such journals as the *American Economic Review*, the *Journal of Political Economy*, the *Review of Economics and Statistics*, *Economica*, and *Research Policy*.

Much of Professor Link's research has been supported by funding organizations such as the National Science Foundation, the Organisation for Economic Co-operation and Development (OECD), the World Bank, and the

DOI: 10.1057/9781137370884

science and technology ministries in several developed nations. Professor Link served as the vice-chairperson of the Innovation and Competitiveness Policies Committee of the United Nation's Economic Commission for Europe (UNECE) from 2007 to 2012.

**John T. Scott** is Professor of Economics at Dartmouth College. He received his Ph.D. in Economics from Harvard University and A.B. in Economics and English from the University of North Carolina at Chapel Hill. His research is in the areas of industrial organization and the economics of technological change. He has served as the President of the Industrial Organization Society and on the editorial boards of the *International Journal of Industrial Organization*, the *Review of Industrial Organization*, and *The Journal of Industrial Economics*. He has also served as an economist at the Board of Governors of the Federal Reserve System and at the Federal Trade Commission. Professor Scott's books include *Market Structure and Technological Change* (1987), *Purposive Diversification and Economic Performance* (1993 and 2005), and *Environmental Research and Development: US Industrial Research, the Clean Air Act and Environmental Damage* (2003). His published research in academic journals has spanned five different decades, and his research about the economics of technological change has been supported by the National Institute of Standards and Technology, the National Science Foundation, the National Research Council of the National Academies, the World Bank, the United Nations Development Programme, and the Organisation for Economic Co-operation and Development.

DOI: 10.1057/9781137370884

palgrave▶**pivot**

www.palgrave.com/pivot

# 1
# Introduction

**Abstract:** *This chapter introduces the monograph as a summary of our research over the past decade on the U.S. Small Business Innovation Research (SBIR) program. The remaining chapters in the monograph are briefly summarized.*

Link, Albert N. and Scott, John T. (2013).
*Bending the Arc of Innovation: Public Support of R&D in Small, Entrepreneurial Firms,*
New York: Palgrave Macmillan, 2013.
DOI: 10.1057/9781137370884.

Entrepreneurial firms are "the engines of American innovation and our [nation's key to] economic success" (White House, 2013a).

> Entrepreneurs embody the promise of America: the idea that if you have a good idea and are willing to work hard and see it through, you can succeed in this country. And in fulfilling this promise, entrepreneurs also play a critical role in expanding our economy and creating jobs.

Research and development (R&D), notably R&D conducted in small, entrepreneurial firms, is fundamental to the development of new technology, and new technology is the driver of innovation. It is well known that private-sector firms—small, entrepreneurial firms, in particular—underinvest in R&D, and thus public support of R&D is both warranted and generally provided.[1]

In this monograph we overview a key national program that supports the development of new technology and innovation in small, entrepreneurial firms. The Small Business Innovation Research (SBIR) program was established by the Small Business Innovation Development Act of 1982 (Public Law 97–219; hereafter, the 1982 Act). In 2000, the National Research Council (NRC) of the National Academies conducted an evaluation study of the economic benefits achieved by the SBIR program. The NRC study was instrumental in bringing about, after several years of temporary extensions of the program, the December 31, 2011 reauthorization of the program.

As part of the NRC study, an extensive and balanced survey of completed SBIR projects was undertaken. We have had the privilege of being able to study the SBIR program over the past decade and to analyze in detail the NRC data over the past seven years. Herein we summarize, for a general audience and for those academics seeking an introductory overview of the SBIR program,[2] many of the findings and conclusions from our extensive analysis.[3] This body of research defines much of the extant literature—certainly all of the recent literature—related to what may be called the economics of the SBIR program.[4]

We conclude from our years of study of the SBIR program that it is indeed bending the arc of innovation. The majority of firms that received SBIR project funding reported that they would not have undertaken the project in the absence of SBIR support. And, it seems clear to us that the SBIR support has had a positive impact on the employment trajectory of firms and on their ability to commercialize innovations resulting from their funded research.

DOI: 10.1057/9781137370884

Before overviewing the remaining chapters of this monograph it is important to draw attention to our use of the term *entrepreneurial* with reference to the firms that received SBIR funding and that we have studied extensively. Throughout intellectual history as we know it, the entrepreneur has worn many hats and played many roles. Thus, a single and well-defined definition of an entrepreneur, or of entrepreneurship meaning what an entrepreneur does, or of a firm being characterized as exhibiting entrepreneurial behavior, is somewhat a matter of debate.

As Hébert and Link (1988, 2006, 2009) have carefully chronicled, the entrepreneur has been thought of variously as: the person who assumes the risk associated with uncertainty, the person who supplies financial capital, an innovator, a decision maker, an industrial leader, a manager or superintendent, an organizer and coordinator of economic resources, the owner of an enterprise, an employer of factors of production, a contractor, an arbitrageur, and an allocator of resources among alternative uses. These are not mutually exclusive characterizations; see Table 1.1 for the names of classical scholars associated with each characterization. The perspective we have adopted when considering firms that have received SBIR funding as being entrepreneurial firms—they are small firms by legislative mandate of the size of a firm that is eligible to apply for a SBIR award—builds specifically on Cantillon's (1931) view of entrepreneurship as action that embraces uncertainty and risk taking, and on Schumpeter's (1928) view of entrepreneurship that embraces innovative action.[5,6]

TABLE 1.1   *Characterizations about 'who the entrepreneur is'*

| An entrepreneur is... | Classical scholar |
|---|---|
| the person who assumes the risk associated with uncertainty | Richard Cantillon |
| the person who supplies financial capital | Adam Smith |
| an innovator | Joseph Schumpeter |
| a decision maker | Carl Menger |
| an industrial leader | J.B. Say |
| a manger or superintendent | John Stuart Mill |
| an organizer and coordinator of economic resources | Léon Walras |
| the owner of an enterprise | François Quesnay |
| an employer of factors of production | Amasa Walker |
| a contractor | Jeremy Bentham |
| an arbitrageur | Israel Kirzner |
| an allocator of resources among alternative uses | T.W. Schultz |

*Source*: Based on Hébert and Link (1988, 2006, 2009).

DOI: 10.1057/9781137370884

The remainder of this monograph is outlined as follows. In Chapter 2, we discuss in general terms market failure as an economic argument for public support of R&D.

In Chapter 3, we motivate the passage of the 1982 Act in terms of a public response to the productivity slowdown in the United States in the early, and then again in the late, 1970s.

Chapter 4 reflects on the early academic research related to small, entrepreneurial firms. Elsewhere (e.g., Link and Scott, 2012a), we have relied on this academic foundation as one motivating factor for the study of small, entrepreneurial firms as well as for the creation of the SBIR program.

The history of the SBIR program is outlined in Chapter 5, and in Chapter 6, we discuss the economic role of the SBIR program.

The foundation for our collective research on the SBIR program comes from economic theory and from our empirical analysis of the NRC database, which is discussed in Chapter 7.

In Chapter 8, we draw directly on our previously published studies related to (1) the probability of a firm commercializing the technology from its SBIR-funded project, (2) employment growth of firms that conducted a SBIR-funded project, and (3) relationships forged with other firms as a result of the developed SBIR-funded technology.

We emphasize in Chapter 8 the findings and conclusions from this body of our research.[7]

We observe in Chapter 9 that there has not yet been a systematic evaluation of the entire SBIR program, the NRC study notwithstanding, and we suggest a method to employ for such an undertaking. We illustrate the method with our evaluation, as a part of an earlier NRC study, of the Department of Defense's (DoD's) SBIR program.

The monograph ends in Chapter 10 with concluding observations about public support of R&D in entrepreneurial firms.

## Notes

1    See Martin and Scott (2000) for a discussion that places such underinvestment in the general context where "[l]imited appropriability, financial market failure, external benefits to the production of knowledge, and other factors suggest that strict reliance on a market system will result in underinvestment in innovation, relative to the socially desirable level.

DOI: 10.1057/9781137370884

This creates a *prima facie* case in favor of public intervention to promote innovative activity" (Martin and Scott, 2000, p. 438).

2   For one introductory overview, see Link and Scott (2012e).

3   We thank Dr. Charles Wessner of the NRC for graciously making the NRC data available to us in support of our academic research.

4   Lerner (1999) provides an important, early examination of the SBIR program.

5   See specifically, Cantillon (1931) and Schumpeter (1928).

6   Link and Link (2009) argued that the establishment of the SBIR program is an example of government acting as an entrepreneur. Government acts as an entrepreneur when its involvement in establishing a technology infrastructure is both innovative and characterized by uncertainty.

7   We refer the reader to our original research for a detailed discussion of the econometric details underlying the general findings that we summarize herein, as well as for complete sets of specific empirical results. Although we draw directly from the text of the original research on a number of occasions, we encourage the learned scholar to refer to the original research for subtle details.

DOI: 10.1057/9781137370884

# 2
# Market Failure and Public Support of R&D

**Abstract:** *This chapter summarizes the economic arguments for public support of private-sector R&D activity. The economic concept of market failure is discussed.*

▶

Link, Albert N. and Scott, John T. (2013). *Bending the Arc of Innovation: Public Support of R&D in Small, Entrepreneurial Firms*, New York: Palgrave Macmillan, 2013. DOI: 10.1057/9781137370884.

DOI: 10.1057/9781137370884

One theoretical basis for public support of R&D to private-sector firms, entrepreneurial firms or otherwise, is the concept of market failure. Market failure, in the context herein, refers to the market—including both the R&D-investing producers of a technology and the users of the technology—underinvesting, from society's standpoint, in a particular technology or technology application. Such underinvestment occurs because conditions exist that prevent firms from fully realizing or appropriating the benefits created by their R&D investments. These conditions are often associated with market power, imperfect information, externalities, and public goods.[1] Drawing directly from Arrow's (1962, pp. 609–610) seminal article on this point:

> We have then three of the classical reasons for the possible failure of perfect competition to achieve optimality in [an innovation-related] resource allocation: indivisibilities, inappropriability, and uncertainty. The first problem has been much studied in the literature under the heading of marginal-cost pricing and the second under that of divergence between social and private benefit (or cost), but the theory of optimal allocation of resources under uncertainty has had much less attention. I will summarize what formal theory exists and then point to the critical notion of information, which arises only in the context of uncertainty. The economic characteristics of information as a commodity and, in particular, of invention as a process for the production of information are next examined. It is shown that all three of the reasons given above for a failure of the competitive system to achieve an optimal resource allocation hold in the case of invention. On theoretical grounds a number of considerations are adduced as to the likely biases in the misallocation and the implications for economic organization.

To elaborate on the concept of market failure, consider a marketable technology to be produced through an R&D process where conditions prevent the R&D-investing firm from fully appropriating the benefits from its technological advancement. Because other firms in the market will realize some of the benefits from the research activities of the R&D-investing firm, and because consumers of goods embodying the research results will pay less than the value they receive,[2] the R&D investing firm will determine that the marginal benefits it can receive from a unit investment in such R&D will be less than it could earn in the absence of the conditions reducing the appropriated benefits. Therefore, the R&D-investing firm will underinvest in R&D, relative to what it would have chosen as its investment in the absence of the conditions. Stated differently, the R&D-investing firm might determine that its private

DOI: 10.1057/9781137370884

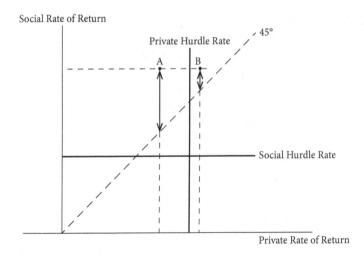

**FIGURE 2.1**    *Spillover gap between social and private rates of return to R&D*
*Source*: Based on Link and Scott (2011, p. 6).

rate of return from its investments in R&D is less than its private hurdle rate—its minimum accepted rate of return—and therefore it would not undertake the socially valuable R&D.

We illustrate this situation conceptually in Figure 2.1. The social rate of return is measured on the vertical axis along with society's hurdle rate on investments in R&D. The private rate of return is measured on the horizontal axis along with the private hurdle rate on investments in R&D. A 45-degree line (dashed) is imposed on the figure under the assumption that the social rate of return from an R&D investment will at least equal the private rate of return from the same level of R&D investment. For illustrative purposes, projects A and B are shown to have the same social rate of return.

The private rate of return is less than the private hurdle rate for project A because the firm cannot fully appropriate the benefits of its R&D investments in that project. As such, it will not choose to invest in project A, although the social benefits from undertaking project A are above the social hurdle rate. Project A is obviously a candidate for public support. In comparison, project B yields the same social rate of return as project A, but the private rate of return is greater than the private hurdle rate because that firm can appropriate the benefits of its R&D investments in that project. Thus, the firm has an incentive to invest in Project B on

DOI: 10.1057/9781137370884

its own even though the social rate of return is greater than the private rate of return. Alternatively stated, there is no economic justification for public resources being allocated to support project B.

The vertical distance shown in Figure 2.1 between the double arrows for the projects is often referred to by the term *spillover gap*. The spillover gap results from the additional value society would receive above what the firm would receive if the R&D project in question were undertaken. The spillover gap could be thought of as a measure of the consequences—a loss of socially valuable benefits in excess of the opportunity costs—of market failure, that is, of the firm not investing in the R&D project.

## Notes

1   The remainder of this chapter draws from Link and Scott (2011, 2012a).
2   Economists refer to this as a gain in consumer surplus.

DOI: 10.1057/9781137370884

# 3
## The Productivity Slowdown in the United States

**Abstract:** *In this chapter the passage of the Small Business Innovation Development Act of 1982, which created the SBIR program, is placed in the context of the U.S. productivity slowdown in the 1970s.*

Link, Albert N. and Scott, John T. (2013).
*Bending the Arc of Innovation: Public Support of R&D in Small, Entrepreneurial Firms,*
New York: Palgrave Macmillan, 2013.
DOI: 10.1057/9781137370884.

DOI: 10.1057/9781137370884

Total factor productivity (TFP) is arguably a measure of technological advancement. TFP is a measure of output relative to a measure of all units of inputs.[1,2] Figure 3.1 shows TFP for the U.S. private business sector for the period 1948 through 2011.[3] Evident from Figure 3.1 is that TFP declined between 1973 and 1974; it increased until 1978 and then generally decreased through 1982. Although there was a productivity slowdown in both time periods, the term *productivity slowdown* generally refers to the 1978–1982 time period.

To put the U.S. productivity slowdown in a global perspective, most industrialized nations, especially those in Europe, experienced slowdowns in measured productivity during similar time periods.

The public sector in the United States, which is the focus of this chapter, responded to these two periods of productivity slowdown—especially the second period—in a number of policy-specific ways including the promulgation of several policies specifically aimed at stimulating technological advancement. These policies included, for example, the University and Small Business Patent Procurement Act of 1980, commonly referred to as the Bayh-Dole Act; the Stevenson-Wydler Technology Innovation Act of 1980, referred to as the Stevenson-Wydler Act; the research and experimentation (R&E) tax credit of 1981;[4] the Small Business Innovation Development Act of 1982, which is discussed in detail below; and the National Cooperative Research Act of 1984.

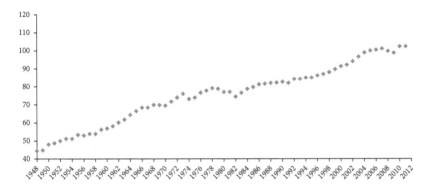

FIGURE 3.1   *Total factor productivity index (2005 = 100)*

*Source:* Based on data from Bureau of Labor Statistics <http://www.bls.gov/mfp/tables.htm>.

DOI: 10.1057/9781137370884

The Bayh-Dole Act and the Stevenson-Wydler Act provided incentives to universities and federal laboratories, respectively, to transfer their in-house technologies to the private sector. The R&E tax credit offered a tax credit to organizations based on the amount that they increased their R&E investments over a base amount; and the National Cooperative Research Act encouraged firms to form research joint ventures to undertake R&D cooperatively. These three initiatives were designed as incentives for the private sector to increase its investments in R&D.

The remainder of this monograph is focused specifically on the Small Business Innovation Development Act, which created the SBIR program, and on our economic research related to various impacts from that program.

## Notes

1   To draw a comparison, labor productivity is measured in terms of output per unit of labor, where labor is one of several factors of production such as capital, energy, and materials.

2   The U.S. Bureau of Labor statistics uses the term *multifactor productivity* (MFP) rather than the term total factor productivity. Details about the calculation of MFP are at <http://www.bls.gov/mfp/mprtech.pdf>.

3   These data come from the Bureau of Labor Statistics <http://www.bls.gov/mfp/tables.htm>.

4   The R&E tax credit was part of the Economic Recovery Tax Act of 1981.

DOI: 10.1057/9781137370884

# 4
# An Emphasis on Small, Entrepreneurial Firms

**Abstract:** *The SBIR program is focused on small, entrepreneurial firms. Arguments supporting a policy emphasis on small, entrepreneurial firms are summarized in this chapter from a historical perspective.*

Link, Albert N. and Scott, John T. (2013).
*Bending the Arc of Innovation: Public Support of R&D in Small, Entrepreneurial Firms,*
New York: Palgrave Macmillan, 2013.
DOI: 10.1057/9781137370884.

Prior to the post-productivity slowdown policy initiatives above, a research report from the Massachusetts Institute of Technology's *Neighborhood and Regional Change* program was independently and coincidently published in 1979.[1] Birch (1979, 1981) concluded in that report that three-fifths of the net new jobs between 1969 and 1976 were created by small firms with 20 or fewer employees. According to Birch (1979, p. 29):

> On average about 60 percent of all jobs in the U.S. are generated by firms with 20 or fewer employees, about 50 percent of all jobs are created by independent, small entrepreneurs. Large firms (those with over 500 employees) generate less than 15 percent of all net new jobs.

Birch (1979) also reported that approximately 80 percent of net new jobs were created by firms with 100 or fewer employees.[2]

Reflecting more broadly than on the productivity slowdown in the early and late 1970s—to some, a period of economic disequilibrium— Schultz (1980, p. 443) noted that:

> [D]isequilibria are inevitable in [any] dynamic economy. These disequilibria cannot be eliminated by law, by public policy, and surely not by rhetoric. A modern dynamic economy would fall apart if not for the entrepreneurial actions of a wide array of human agents who reallocate their resources [to form new combinations] and thereby bring their part of the economy back into equilibrium.

One might think of the productivity recovery that began in the early 1980s in terms of entrepreneurial responses to disequilibria. Or, using the terms of Audretsch and Thurik (2001, 2004), the recovery from the productivity slowdown reflects the end of the era of the *Managed Economy* (with predictable outputs coming from an established manufacturing sector) and the emergence of the *Entrepreneurial Economy*.

In the *Entrepreneurial Economy*, characterized by the emergence of economic agents embodied with entrepreneurial capital, smaller firms have a greater ability to be innovative, or to adopt and adapt others' new technologies and ideas, and thus quickly and efficiently appropriate investments in new knowledge that are made externally.

According to Audretsch and Thurik (2004, p. 144), with an emphasis on small firms within the *Entrepreneurial Economy*: "entrepreneurship has emerged [during the late 1970s] as the engine of economic and social development throughout the world."

Given the insights in the scholarly studies about entrepreneurship, perhaps it is not surprising that policy makers toward the end of the

DOI: 10.1057/9781137370884

1970s embraced small, entrepreneurial firms as engines of future economic growth.

There are at least two explanations for this shift in policy emphasis toward small, entrepreneurial firms (Carlsson, 1992). First, there had been a fundamental change in the world economy beginning in the mid-1970s. Global competition was increasing, markets were becoming less fragmented, and the factors viewed as determinants of future economic growth were uncertain. Thus, entrepreneurial leadership adjusted to this disequilibrium, and the policy changes reflected an appreciation of the economic engine entrepreneurship powered. Second, and related, flexible automation was being introduced throughout the manufacturing sector, thus reducing economies of scale as a barrier for entry into many markets and thereby opening the door for smaller, entrepreneurial firms to enter and succeed.

Economic conditions were, as we look back through an interpretative lens on that time period, right for the policy environment in the late-1970s and early-1980s to be receptive to the establishment of the SBIR program.

## Notes

1  The remainder of this chapter draws from Link and Scott (2012a).

2  In subsequent research, Birch (1987) found that small businesses with less than 20 employees accounted for 88 percent of all net new jobs over the period 1981–1985. Also, according to Birch (1981, p. 7), "Smaller businesses more than offset their higher failure rates with their capacity to start up and expand rapidly."

DOI: 10.1057/9781137370884

# 5
# The SBIR Program

**Abstract:** *The legislative history of the SBIR program is summarized in this chapter, and the government agencies that participate in the program are described.*

▶ Link, Albert N. and Scott, John T. (2013). *Bending the Arc of Innovation: Public Support of R&D in Small, Entrepreneurial Firms,* New York: Palgrave Macmillan, 2013. DOI: 10.1057/9781137370884.

DOI: 10.1057/9781137370884

The SBIR program is a public/private partnership that provides research grants to fund identified private-sector R&D projects.[1] The research grants are intended to help fulfill the government's mission to enhance private-sector R&D and to complement federal research needs of research.[2]

A prototype of the SBIR program began at the National Science Foundation (NSF) in 1977 (Tibbetts, 1999). At that time, the goal of the program was to encourage small businesses—increasingly recognized by the policy community to be a source of innovation and employment in the U.S. economy—to participate in NSF-sponsored research, especially research with commercial potential. Because of the early success of the program at NSF, Congress passed the Small Business Innovation Development Act of 1982 (Public Law 97–219), or as simply referred to herein, the 1982 Act.[3]

The 1982 Act required all government departments and agencies with external research programs of greater than $100 million to establish internally their own SBIR program and to set aside funds equal to 0.20 percent of the external research budget.[4] To provide a benchmark against which subsequent totals can be compared, observe that in 1983 that set aside totaled $45 million.

The 1982 Act stated that the objectives of the program are:

1  to stimulate technological innovation,
2  to use small business to meet Federal research and development needs,
3  to foster and encourage participation by minority and disadvantaged persons in technological innovation, and
4  to increase private-sector commercialization of innovations derived from Federal research and development.

As part of the 1982 Act, SBIR program awards were structured and defined by three phases. Phase I awards were small, generally less than $50,000 for the six-month award period.[5] The purpose of Phase I awards was and still is to assist businesses as they assess the feasibility of an idea's scientific and commercial potential in response to the funding agency's objectives.[6] Phase II awards were capped at $500,000; they generally lasted for two years. These awards were and still are for the business to develop further its proposed research, ideally leading to a commercializable product, process, or service.[7] The Phase II awards of public funds for development are sometimes augmented by outside private funding (Wessner, 2000). Further work on the projects launched through the

DOI: 10.1057/9781137370884

SBIR program occurs in what is called Phase III, which does not involve SBIR funds.[8] At this stage, firms needing additional financing—to ensure that the product, process, or service can move into the marketplace—are expected to obtain it from sources other than the SBIR program.

As stated in the 1982 Act, to be eligible for a SBIR award, the small business must be independently owned and operated; other than the dominant firm in the field in which it is proposing to carry out SBIR projects; organized and operated for profit; the employer of 500 or fewer employees, including employees of subsidiaries and affiliates; the primary source of employment for the project's principal investigator at the time of award and during the period when the research is conducted; and at least 51 percent owned by U.S. citizens or lawfully admitted permanent resident aliens.

In 1986, the 1982 Act was extended through 1992 as a part of the Department of Defense Appropriation Act of 1986 (Public Law 99–443).

In 1992, the SBIR program was reauthorized again until 2000 through the Small Business Research and Development Enactment Act (Public Law 102–564).

Under the 1982 Act, the set aside had increased to 1.25 percent; the 1992 reauthorization raised that amount over time to 2.50 percent and re-emphasized the commercialization intent of SBIR-funded technologies (see point (4) from the 1982 Act above).[9] The reauthorization also increased Phase I awards to $100,000 and Phase II awards to $750,000.[10] The 1992 reauthorization broadened objective (3) above to also focus on women: "to provide for enhanced outreach efforts to increase the participation of…small businesses that are 51 percent owned and controlled by women."

The Small Business Reauthorization Act of 2000 (Public Law 106–554) extended the SBIR program until September 30, 2008 and kept the 2.50 percent set aside. It retained the 2.50 percent set aside and did not increase the amounts of Phase I and Phase II awards.[11]

Congress did not reauthorize the SBIR program by the legislated date of September 30, 2008; rather, Congress temporarily extended the program until March 20, 2009 (Public Law 110–235). The Senate version of the reauthorization bill (S. 3029) included, among other things, an increase in Phase I funding to $150,000 and an increase in Phase II funding to $1,000,000 with provisions for these funding guidelines to be exceeded by 50 percent. Also, the current 2.50 percent set aside would increase to 3.50 percent at a rate of 0.10 percent per year over 10

DOI: 10.1057/9781137370884

years, except for the National Institutes of Health which would stay at 2.50 percent.

On March 19, 2009, the House and Senate reauthorized the SBIR program until July 31, 2009 (Public Law 110–10); it was again reauthorized to September 30, 2009 through a Senate continuing resolution (S. 1513); on September 23, 2009 a House bill (H.R. 3614) extended SBIR until October 31, 2009; a Senate bill (S. 1929) again extended the program until April 30, 2010; bill (S. 3253) extended the program to July 31; bill (H.R. 5849) extended the program to September 30, 2010; and bills (S. 3839 and H.R. 366) extended the program to January 31 and then May 31, 2011, respectively.[12]

Still to be decided at that time was whether the existing Phase I, Phase II, and Phase III process should remain, whether the dollar size of Phase I and Phase II awards should be changed, and whether venture capitalists should be involved in the SBIR process. While this debate lingered in Congress, the Small Business Administration (SBA) on March 30, 2010 amended the SBIR Policy Directive to allow the threshold amount for Phase I awards to increase to $150,000 and to $1,000,000 for Phase II awards (as was proposed in the Senate version of the reauthorization bill).

On May 31, 2011, the program was yet again temporarily extended through September 30, 2011 by S. 1082, The Small Business Additional Extension Act of 2011. H.R. 2608 extended the program until November 18, 2011; H.R. 2112 extended it again until December 16, 2011. On December 15, 2011 the program was reauthorized by Congress, and on December 31, 2011, President Obama signed the National Defense Authorization Act of 2012 (Public Law 112–81). That act codified the reauthorization of the SBIR program to September 30, 2017.[13]

Thus, after many multi-month extensions of the program because the U.S. Congress failed to reauthorize it in 2008, the SBIR program was eventually reauthorized for six years.

The major legislations leading to the December 31, 2011 authorization are summarized in Table 5.1.

The December 31, 2011 legislation reauthorizing the SBIR program introduced some controversial changes including, for the first time, the provision that small firms that are majority-owned by venture capital operating companies, hedge funds, or private equity firms are eligible to participate in the program.

DOI: 10.1057/9781137370884

TABLE 5.1   *Major legislation related to the SBIR program*

| Legislation | Public Law | Relevant time period |
|---|---|---|
| Small Business Innovation Development Act of 1982 | Public Law 97–219 | 1982–1986 |
| Department of Defense Appropriation Act of 1986 | Public Law 99–443 | 1986–1992 |
| Small Business Research and Development Enactment Act of 1992 | Public Law 102–564 | 1992–2000 |
| Small Business Reauthorization Act of 2000 | Public Law 106–554 | 2000–2008 |
| *Temporary Extensions* | | 2008–2012 |
| National Defense Authorization Act of 2012 | Public Law 112–81 | 2012–2017 |

*Source*: Prepared by the authors.

Eleven agencies currently participate in the SBIR program: the Environmental Protection Agency (EPA), National Aeronautics and Space Administration (NASA), National Science Foundation (NSF), and the Departments of Agriculture (USDA), Commerce (DoC), Defense (DoD), Education (ED), Energy (DOE), Health and Human Services (HHS, particularly NIH), Transportation (DoT), and, most recently, Homeland Security (DHS).

In 2005 (the year of the survey from which the studies summarized in Chapter 8 come), DoD maintained the largest program, awarding about 51 percent of the $1.85 billion dollars of Phase I and Phase II funding, and about 57 percent of 5,873 Phase I and Phase II awards in that year. Five agencies—DoD, HHS, NASA, DOE, and NSF—account for nearly 97 percent of the program's expenditures, with HHS (which includes the NIH) being the second most important, accounting for 30 percent of total dollars and 19 percent of awards in 2005. SBIR Phase II awards from these five agencies are the focus of the studies that we conducted that are summarized in Chapter 8.

Representative examples of Phase II projects funded by DoD, NIH, NASA, DOE, and NSF are presented in Appendix A.

# Notes

1   Every year, each agency's SBIR program solicits applications for research on a set of predetermined topics to meet its research needs. See stated

DOI: 10.1057/9781137370884

objective (2) below from the Small Business Innovation Development Act of 1982.

2   This chapter draws on Link and Scott (2000, 2012a); Audretsch, Link, and Scott (2002); and Wessner (2000, 2008).

3   The 1982 Act amended the Small Business Act of 1953 (Public Law 85–536) which established the Small Business Administration.

4   SBIR is a set aside program; it redirects existing R&D funds for competitive awards to small businesses rather than appropriating new monies for R&D. The 1982 Act allowed for this percentage to increase over time.

5   The $50,000 amount and the $500,000 amount below are not stated in the 1982 Act. They originally came from a Policy Directive to the Small Business Act of 1953, to which the 1982 Act was an amendment. Both amounts are referenced explicitly in the U.S. Senate Report 110–447 (2008).

6   "The objective of Phase I is to determine the technical merit, feasibility, and commercial potential of the proposed research or R/R&D efforts and to determine the quality of performance of the small business awardee organization prior to providing further Federal support in Phase II." See http://www.sbir.gov/about/about-sbir]

7   "The objective of Phase II is to continue the R/R&D efforts initiated in Phase I. Funding is based on the results achieved in Phase I and the scientific and technical merit and commercial potential of the project proposed in Phase II." See http://www.sbir.gov/about/about-sbir

8   "The objective of Phase III, where appropriate, is for the small business to pursue commercialization objectives resulting from the Phase I/II R/R&D activities." See http://www.sbir.gov/about/about-sbir.

9   The percentage increased to 1.50 in 1993 and 1994, 2.00 in 1995, and 2.50 in 1997.

10  The reauthorization also stated that there should be an "adjustment of such amounts once every 5 years to reflect economic adjustments and economic considerations." Such adjustments have not occurred.

11  It had not been uncommon for Phase II awards to exceed the $750,000 threshold.

12  On October 7, 2009 the House and Senate Armed Services Committees recommended that the DoD SBIR program be reauthorized for a year, until September 30, 2010. This recommendation became part of the Department of Defense 2010 Authorization.

13  For additional information on the reauthorization and its legislative changes, see Schacht (2012).

DOI: 10.1057/9781137370884

# 6

# The Economic Role of the SBIR Program

**Abstract:** *A model of downside risk is posited as an economic rationale for the SBIR program. The model is developed and illustrated in this chapter.*

Link, Albert N. and Scott, John T. (2013).
*Bending the Arc of Innovation: Public Support of R&D in Small, Entrepreneurial Firms,*
New York: Palgrave Macmillan, 2013.
DOI: 10.1057/9781137370884.

DOI: 10.1057/9781137370884

The SBIR program is often characterized with reference to the Valley of Death. According to Branscomb and Auerswald (2002, p. 35), with reference to Figure 6.1:[1]

> [The Valley of Death] suggests a barren territory. In reality, however, between the stable shores of the science and technology enterprise and the business and finance enterprise is a sea of life and death of business and technical ideas, of big fish and little fish contending, with survival going to the creative, the agile, the persistent.

SBIR funding, as well as other sources of funding that we discuss below using our own research, helps a firm transcend the Valley of Death by providing funding to bridge (as shown in Figure 6.1) the gap between a potential technology and a commercializable innovation.

From a more narrowly economic perspective, the role of the SBIR program is illustrated in Figure 6.2 in terms of risk reduction.[2] Rate of return, r, is measured on the horizontal axis and the probability density for that rate of return, f(r), is measured on the vertical axis. The reduction in risk resulting from a SBIR award is shown as a rightward shift in the distribution of the rate of return for the private firms. The rightward shift of the distribution, and the concept of reducing the probability of returns lower than acceptable to the private investors, applies equally well to the absolute level of net return (absolute return minus private

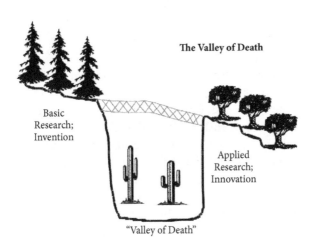

The Valley of Death

Basic
Research;
Invention

Applied
Research;
Innovation

"Valley of Death"

**FIGURE 6.1**   *An image of the Valley of Death*
Source: Based on Branscomb and Auerswald (2002, p. 36).

DOI: 10.1057/9781137370884

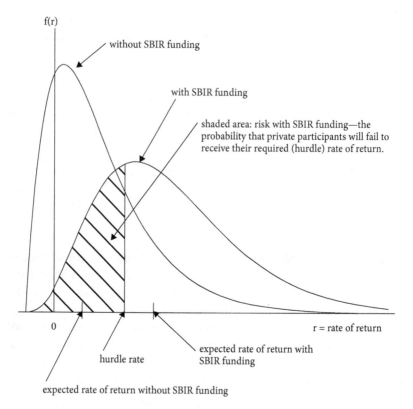

**FIGURE 6.2**    *Private risk reduction resulting from SBIR funding*
*Source*: Based on Link and Scott (2010, p. 592; 2012a, p. 27).

investment) expected from the project. As shown in the figure, SBIR support increases the firm's expected private rate of return and thereby reduces the downside risk associated with undertaking R&D. For each distribution—without SBIR funding (left distribution) and with SBIR funding (right distribution)—the expected rate of return is labeled. As shown in Figure 6.2, with SBIR funding the expected private rate of return and the variance in the private rate of return from the research project will increase.

Consider the left distribution in Figure 6.2—the distribution of the rate of return for a project considered by a private firm without SBIR funding. As drawn, the private hurdle rate is to the right of the project's expected rate of return without SBIR funding, meaning that the private

DOI: 10.1057/9781137370884

firm will not undertake this research project because the firm will not receive its required rate of return. This project is comparable to project A in Figure 2.1. The risk of undertaking this project equals the area under the without-SBIR distribution that is to the left of the private hurdle rate.[3] Consider the distribution to the right in Figure 6.2—the distribution of the rate of return for the private firm's project with SBIR funding. With SBIR funding, the private firm will expect on its project a rate of return greater than its hurdle rate—the expected private rate of return with SBIR funding is therefore to the right of the private hurdle rate. While SBIR funding will not itself increase the probability that the research project will be successful, assuming hypothetically that it were undertaken absent SBIR funding, it will however reduce private risk by increasing the expected private rate of return because the expected rate of return will be based on a smaller private outlay. Thus, SBIR funding leverages the private firm's investment as illustrated by a greater expected return and a greater variance in the distribution as explained above. Stated differently, SBIR support to the firm bends its arc of innovation—that is, the trajectory of the firm's innovation path is changed by the SBIR program.

The hashed area in Figure 6.2 is what we call the downside risk of the project; it is the probability that the project will yield a rate of return less than the private hurdle rate even with SBIR funding. Hence, the amount of downside risk with SBIR funding is visually less than the downside risk associated with the research project in the without-SBIR funding case.

Although we are comfortable with our conclusion from Figure 6.2 that SBIR funding reduces risk—as defined operationally in terms of reducing the probability of a rate of return below the private hurdle rate—we do emphasize that our argument is in no way dependant on any particular measure of risk or any particular model of capital asset pricing with associated systematic and non-systematic risk. Instead, our treatment encompasses any and all such models because the relevant risk, however it is perceived by private firms, is captured in the private hurdle rate, and the distributions of returns are otherwise represented by their expected values. In describing the effect of SBIR funding on the distribution of private rates of return, we are describing an underlying reality that would be reflected in the private hurdle rate—as determined by some model—and in the expected value of the returns.

DOI: 10.1057/9781137370884

## Notes

1   This diagram is attributed by Branscomb and Auerswald (2002) to Congressman Ehlers (2000).

2   This chapter, with reference to the discussion about Figure 6.2, draws from Link and Scott (2010, 2012a).

3   For those who are used to thinking of the variance of the distribution as the measure of risk, the downside risk—which is the probability of a rate of return less than the hurdle rate—might seem unusual. Variance measures the possibility that outcomes can differ from the expected outcome, while the downside risk measures the probability of an outcome departing to the downside of the hurdle rate. Note that the technical risk and the market risk for the project are reflected in the variance of the distribution—the technical goals may exceed or fall short of expectations and market acceptance of the project's technical outcomes could do the same. The downside risk refers to the outcomes that fall short of the hurdle rate.

DOI: 10.1057/9781137370884

# 7
# The National Research Council Database

**Abstract:** *Empirical analyses related to the SBIR program are based on the National Research Council's database of Phase II awards. The history of the database is described in this chapter along with descriptive statistics.*

Link, Albert N. and Scott, John T. (2013).
*Bending the Arc of Innovation: Public Support of R&D in Small, Entrepreneurial Firms,*
New York: Palgrave Macmillan, 2013.
DOI: 10.1057/9781137370884.

The Small Business Reauthorization Act of 2000 mandated that, among other things, the NRC conduct: "an evaluation of the economic benefits achieved by the SBIR program [and make recommendations to Congress for] improvements to the SBIR program."

In its evaluation of the SBIR program, the NRC conducted an extensive and balanced survey in 2005 based on a population of 11,214 projects completed from Phase II awards made between 1992 and 2001 by five agencies: DoD, NIH within HHS, NASA, DOE, and NSF. It was assumed as part of the NRC's sampling methodology that Phase II awards made in 2001 would be completed by 2005.

As noted above, the five agencies surveyed accounted for nearly 97 percent of the program's expenditures in 2005, the year of the survey. Table 7.1 shows the distribution of the population of 11,214 projects by funding agency, and the percentage of the 11,214 projects funded by each agency. The total number of projects surveyed from the 11,214 population of projects was 6,408.

TABLE 7.1    *Population of SBIR Phase II projects 1992–2001*

| Agency | Completed Phase II projects | Percentage |
|--------|-----------------------------|------------|
| DoD    | 5,650                       | 50.38      |
| NIH    | 2,497                       | 22.27      |
| NASA   | 1,488                       | 13.27      |
| DOE    | 808                         | 7.21       |
| NSF    | 771                         | 6.88       |
|        | 11,214                      | 100.00     |

*Source*: Based on Link and Scott (2012a, p. 34; 2012b, p. 6).

TABLE 7.2    *Descriptive statistics on the National Research Council Survey of Phase II awards*

| Agency | Phase II sample size | Respondents | Response rate (%) | Random sample |
|--------|----------------------|-------------|-------------------|---------------|
| DoD    | 3,055                | 920         | 30                | 891           |
| NIH    | 1,678                | 496         | 30                | 495           |
| NASA   | 779                  | 181         | 23                | 177           |
| DOE    | 439                  | 157         | 36                | 154           |
| NSF    | 457                  | 162         | 35                | 161           |
|        | 6,408                | 1,916       | 30                | 1,878         |

*Source*: Based on Link and Scott (2012a, p. 35; 2012b, p. 6).

DOI: 10.1057/9781137370884

The number and percentage of respondents from these 6,408 projects surveyed by the NRC is shown in Table 7.2. The total number of responding projects was 1,916, and the average response rate across all five agencies was about 30 percent. Also shown in Table 7.2 is the total number of projects in the final random sample of completed Phase II projects, by agency. See Figure 7.1 for the percentage of the random sample funded by each agency.

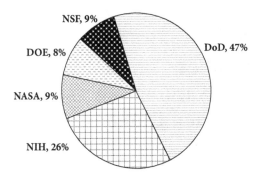

FIGURE 7.1    *Percentage of the random sample funded, by agency*
Source: Prepared by the authors.

DOI: 10.1057/9781137370884

# 8

# Studies Conducted Using the National Research Council Database

**Abstract:** *Three areas of literature are summarized in this chapter. They relate to the (1) probability of a firm commercializing from a SBIR-funded project, (2) employment growth in firms that conducted a SBIR-funded project, and (3) relationships with other firms forged from SBIR-funded projects.*

Link, Albert N. and Scott, John T. (2013).
*Bending the Arc of Innovation: Public Support of R&D in Small, Entrepreneurial Firms,*
New York: Palgrave Macmillan, 2013.
DOI: 10.1057/9781137370884.

DOI: 10.1057/9781137370884

We conducted a number of studies using the NRC database. These studies broadly fall within three areas:

▶ probability of a firm commercializing from its SBIR-funded project,
▶ employment growth of firms that conducted a SBIR-funded project, and
▶ relationships forged with other firms as a result of the developed SBIR-funded technology.

Before discussing these three areas of our research, some general descriptive information about SBIR-funded projects, calculated from the NRC database, are presented (see Table 8.1). However, we caution one from overly interpreting differences across agencies from this descriptive information, or even from the more detailed information below. As Wessner (2008, p. 109) noted:

> Comparisons between SBIR programs at different agencies…must be regarded with considerable caution.… [W]idely differing agency missions have shaped the agency SBIR programs, focusing them on different objectives and on different mechanisms and approaches. [For example, agencies] whose mission is to develop technologies for internal agency use via procurement [e.g., DoD] have a quite different orientation from agencies that do not procure technology and are instead focused on developing technologies for use outside the agency.

As stated above, Phase II awards at the time that the NRC database was constructed were typically capped at $750,000. On average, across agencies, the level of the Phase II awards was below that cap. DoD awards were, on average, the largest, and NSF awards were, on average, the smallest. On average, the age of the recipient firms was about 11 years.

As mentioned above, the objective of SBIR awards was broadened under the 1992 reauthorization "to provide for enhanced outreach efforts to increase the participation of…small businesses that are 51 percent owned and controlled by women." However, on average, less than 20 percent of projects awarded between 1992 and 2001, the range of years of awards covered by the NRC database, were given to female-owned firms. In fact, less than 10 percent of the DOE and NSF awards went to female-owned firms. Of course, relevant to a more complete assessment of the effect of the 1992 objective would be a comparison to the percentage of projects that went to female-owned firms before 1992; such data would be useful, but they are not available.

DOI: 10.1057/9781137370884

TABLE 8.1  *Descriptive statistics about SBIR-funded firms, means**

| Variable | DoD (n = 755) | NIH (n = 391) | NASA (n = 155) | DOE (n = 140) | NSF (n = 141) |
|---|---|---|---|---|---|
| SBIR award amount ($1,000) | $719.0 | $654.0 | $567.0 | $683.0 | $376.0 |
| Age of the firm (years) at the time of the award | 11.61 | 9.32 | 12.81 | 11.74 | 10.67 |
| Percentage of awards to female-owned firms** | 11.3 | 16.6 | 11.9 | 7.8 | 8.1 |
| Number of founders of the firm with academic background | 1.08 | 1.33 | 1.18 | 1.12 | 1.14 |
| Number of founders of the firm with business background | 0.69 | 0.66 | 0.68 | 0.64 | 0.73 |
| Percentage of projects that were commercialized*** | 45.6 | 49.0 | 45.8 | 52.6 | 49.3 |
| Employees at the time of the award | 35.46 | 20.50 | 45.66 | 33.14 | 23.54 |
| Employees in 2005 | 59.93 | 60.41 | 62.54 | 55.71 | 40.99 |
| Employees hired for the SBIR project | 2.25 | 2.80 | 1.08 | 1.39 | 1.47 |
| Employees retained after completion of the SBIR project | 2.00 | 2.34 | 1.37 | 1.38 | 1.96 |
| Percentage of projects involving a university as a research partner | 25.8 | 52.9 | 30.1 | 38.2 | 51.1 |
| Percentage of projects to commercialize as software | 21.6 | 27.6 | 14.2 | 13.6 | 24.1 |
| Percentage of projects to commercialize as hardware | 39.7 | 25.6 | 43.2 | 41.4 | 39.7 |
| Percentage of projects to commercialize as a process technology | 15.6 | 9.7 | 13.6 | 23.6 | 21.3 |
| Percentage of projects to commercialize as service capability | 12.0 | 11.2 | 12.3 | 15.7 | 15.6 |
| Percentage of projects to commercialize as a drug | — | 1.8 | — | — | — |
| Percentage of projects to commercialize as a biologic | — | 3.8 | — | — | — |
| Percentage of projects to commercialize as a research tool | 10.5 | 26.3 | 14.8 | 10.7 | 15.6 |
| Percentage of projects to commercialize as educational material | 14.6 | 14.6 | 3.2 | 2.9 | 9.2 |

*Sources:* * The means are based on a subset of the random sample used in the employment growth studies summarized below. See Link and Scott (2012a, Table A.2, pp. 116–124). ** The percentages are based on the entire random sample. See Table 7.2. *** The percentages are based on the analysis in Link and Scott (2010, p. 595).

DOI: 10.1057/9781137370884

Prior to the construction of the NRC database, there were no systematic data available on the background of the founders, or entrepreneurs, of SBIR-funded firms. As shown in Table 8.1, on average, it is more likely than not that a SBIR-funded firm would have been founded by an entrepreneur with an academic background than with a business background.

Recall that an objective of the SBIR program is for the firm to commercialize the funded technology. Across funding agencies, the percentage of Phase II projects that are commercialized is visibly similar ranging from 45.6 among DoD-funded projects to 52.3 among DOE-funded projects.

Clearly, from the mean values in Table 8.1, funded firms are small and well below the 500-employee threshold. Across all agencies, the average number of employees at the time the firm received SBIR funding was less than 50. Across all agencies, the average number of employees in 2005—the year that the NRC survey was administered—was greater than the average number of employees at the time the firm's project was funded. Of course, some of this overall growth in employees is due to, among other things, difference in the year of funding and other non-SBIR-related factors associated with the firm's overall growth.

On average, funded firms hired roughly two new employees in response to the SBIR award, and about two employees were retained, on average, at the completion of the project.[1]

On average about 40 percent of the funded projects involved a university, in one way or another, as a research partner. The motivation for university partnerships is ambiguous, and it will be discussed below in terms of employment growth associated with SBIR funding. As Hall, Link, and Scott (2000, 2003) noted, the literature has identified two broad industry motivations for engaging in an industry/university research relationship. The first is access to complementary research activity and research results. More specifically, academic research augments the capacity of businesses to solve complex problems. The second industry motivation is access to key university personnel. University motivations for partnering with industry seem to be financially based. Administration-based financial pressures for faculty to engage in applied commercial research with industry have long been growing.[2] However, there are drawbacks to university involvement with industry R&D, such as the diversion of faculty time and effort from teaching, the conflict between industrial trade secrecy and traditional academic openness, and the distorting effect of industry funding on the university budget allocation process

DOI: 10.1057/9781137370884

TABLE 8.2    *Responses to the counterfactual question: "In your opinion, in the absence of this SBIR award, would your firm have undertaken this project?"*

Percentage and number of the 593 DoD projects (in the random sample) that answered

| Answer | Percentage | Number |
| --- | --- | --- |
| Definitely yes | 3.04 | 18 |
| Probably yes | 9.61 | 57 |
| Uncertain | 17.71 | 105 |
| Probably not | 32.72 | 194 |
| Definitely not | 36.93 | 219 |
| Sum | 100.00 | 593 |

Percentage and number of the 338 NIH projects (in the random sample) that answered

| Answer | Percentage | Number |
| --- | --- | --- |
| Definitely yes | 5.03 | 17 |
| Probably yes | 7.69 | 26 |
| Uncertain | 13.61 | 46 |
| Probably not | 27.81 | 94 |
| Definitely not | 45.86 | 155 |
| Sum | 100.00 | 338 |

Percentage and number of the 111 NASA projects (in the random sample) that answered

| Answer | Percentage | Number |
| --- | --- | --- |
| Definitely yes | 2.70 | 3 |
| Probably yes | 15.32 | 17 |
| Uncertain | 14.41 | 16 |
| Probably not | 35.14 | 39 |
| Definitely not | 32.43 | 36 |
| Sum | 100.00 | 111 |

Percentage and number of the 114 DOE projects (in the random sample) that answered

| Answer | Percentage | Number |
| --- | --- | --- |
| Definitely yes | 0.00 | 0 |
| Probably yes | 3.51 | 4 |
| Uncertain | 13.16 | 15 |
| Probably not | 44.74 | 51 |
| Definitely not | 38.60 | 44 |
| Sum | 100.00 | 114 |

*Continued*

DOI: 10.1057/9781137370884

TABLE 8.2   *Continued*

Percentage and number of the 121 NSF projects (in the random sample) that answered

| Answer | Percentage | Number |
|---|---|---|
| Definitely yes | 3.31 | 4 |
| Probably yes | 12.40 | 15 |
| Uncertain | 18.18 | 22 |
| Probably not | 42.15 | 51 |
| Definitely not | 23.97 | 29 |
| Sum | 100.00 | 121 |

*Note*:  Not all firms that were asked to complete the NRC survey responded to this question.

*Source*:  Based on Link and Scott (2012a, p. 41).

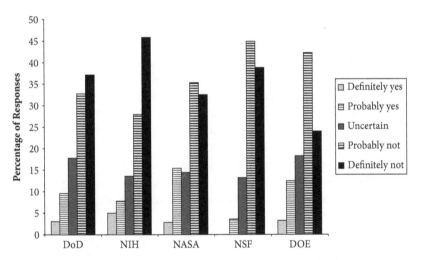

FIGURE 8.1   *Likelihood of a project being started without SBIR funding*
*Source*:  Prepared by the authors.

(in particular, the tension induced when the distribution of resources is vastly unequal across departments and schools).

Lastly, some general observations about how firms expect to commercialize from their SBIR-research can be gleaned from Table 8.1. In particular, across agencies, most projects have or are expected to commercialize as hardware, a final product, component, or intermediate hardware product; only projects funded by NIH have or are expected to commercialize as a drug or a biologic; and few projects have or are expected to commercialize as educational material.

Before describing our findings from the three areas of study noted above in more detail, there are data in the NRC database that allow us to glean insight about the importance of SBIR funding to help the firm transcend the Valley of Death. Table 8.2 and Figure 8.1 show that more often than not, the funded firm would not (i.e., probably not or definitely not) have undertaken its research project in the absence of SBIR support. In fact, only about 3 percent of responding firms reported that they definitely would have undertaken the research project in the absence of SBIR support.

## Commercializing from SBIR-funded projects

An explicit objective of the 1982 Act that established the SBIR program was "to increase private sector commercialization of innovations derived from Federal research and development."

We (Link and Scott, 2010) modeled the probability of commercialization of a SBIR-funded project in terms of all of the information available in the NRC database. That information fell broadly into four categories of variables: non-SBIR funding including outside private investments (e.g., receipt of U.S. private venture capital), Phase II project variables (e.g., award amount), firm variables (e.g., revenue of the firm), and geographic variables (e.g., regional location of the firm). Of particular interest was the independent impact of outside private investments on the probability of commercialization.

Based on our earlier work (Link and Scott, 2009), we hypothesized that outside investments should be positively correlated with the probability of success for at least two reasons. First, outside private investors have useful information about the potentially commercializable outputs of a Phase II project, and by investing in a project those investors signal such information. Second, outside private investors often bring useful managerial guidance to small, entrepreneurial endeavors.

Table 8.3 shows the categories of private investments that are correlated with the probability of commercial success, by funding agency. In all five agencies, some type of outside finance had a significantly positive impact on the probability of commercialization. Funding from other U.S. firms and also the firm's own funding had statistically

DOI: 10.1057/9781137370884

TABLE 8.3    *Categories of private investments that have a statistically significant positive impact on the probability of commercialization*

| Agency | Categories of private investments |
|---|---|
| DoD | U.S. private venture capital |
| | Other private equity |
| | Other U.S. firm funding |
| | Own firm funding |
| NIH | U.S. private venture capital |
| | Own firm funding |
| | Personal funds |
| NASA | Other private equity |
| | Other U.S. firm funding |
| DOE | Other U.S. firm funding |
| | Own firm funding |
| | Personal funds |
| NSF | Other private equity |
| | Other U.S. firm funding |
| | Own firm funding |

*Source*: Summarized from Link and Scott (2010).

significant positive impacts for the SBIR projects of four agencies. Also, for four agencies, U.S. private venture capital or other private equity or both had statistically significant positive impacts on the probability of commercialization.

Table 8.4 shows the predicted probabilities of commercialization, by funding agency. The probabilities shown are the average of the probabilities predicted for each of the sampled SBIR projects with variables set at their actual values for each project. In all cases, the predicted average probability is slightly less than 0.50, or it is slightly less than the probability of a heads on the toss of a fair coin.

Independent of the specific average probabilities of commercialization in Table 8.1 or the predicted probabilities in Table 8.4, we (Link and Scott, 2009) have suggested that the use of a prediction market could improve the commercialization performance of the program.[3]

Consider the following winner-take-all or all-or-nothing contract offered in a SBIR prediction market.

For each Phase I SBIR project that is to be invited by the funding agency to apply for a Phase II award, the agency could issue a block of tradable securities with each security having a face value of, say, $1,000.

DOI: 10.1057/9781137370884

TABLE 8.4    *Predicted probability of commercialization*

| Agency | n | Mean predicted probability of commercialization | Standard. Dev. | Min. | Max. |
|---|---|---|---|---|---|
| DoD | 761 | 0.4480 | 0.3430 | 0.00926 | 1.00 |
| NIH | 382 | 0.4957* | 0.2967 | 0.01889 | 1.00 |
| NASA | 155 | 0.4679 | 0.3901 | 0.0005967 | 1.00 |
| DOE | 131 | 0.4928 | 0.3457 | 0.000702 | 1.00 |
| NSF | 123 | 0.4791 | 0.3514 | 0.0000406 | 1.00 |

* Estimated probability conditional on selection.
*Source*: Based on Link and Scott (2010, p. 600).

The securities promise to pay the face value if the Phase II award were granted and if the resulting project commercializes a product, process, or service by a pre-defined date. Of course, prediction market participants would have to have access to the Phase II application.

The size of an initial Phase II award had typically been on the order of $750,000, so a block of, say, 100 securities with face value $1,000 each would represent a modest investment by the agency in each project— just 13.33 percent of the typical initial grant. This payout amount would be an upper bound on the agency's liability, offset by revenues from the sale of the securities. Further, if the prediction market serves to increase the probability of commercialization because it allows the agency to better select Phase II award recipients, there would be additional social benefits from the SBIR program more frequently meeting its commercialization goal.

Suppose the agency invited two firms with completed Phase I projects to apply for a Phase II award, and suppose that the securities traded in the prediction market for one of those proposed Phase II projects had a market value of $560 while the other had a market value of $230. Roughly speaking, if the discount rate equaled zero, the market is indicating that the probability of commercial success is 0.56 for the one project and 0.23 for the other. At those probabilities, a risk-neutral purchaser of the securities expects the value of the securities to equal their price. Such investors would want to purchase the securities, bidding up their prices from $560 and $230 if the expected probabilities of commercialization were higher; they would want to sell, creating excess supply of the securities and causing prices to fall, if the expected probabilities were lower. Thus, the market prices determined by the trading of the SBIR prediction-market

DOI: 10.1057/9781137370884

securities provide insight into the likelihood of commercialization of the different Phase II projects; theoretically the distribution of prices could be used to determine Phase II funding priorities.

The idea that the prices determined in a well-specified prediction market for winner-take-all contracts reflect the probability of an event, and that collections of such contracts can be used to develop even more information about the parameters of the probability distribution for a future event, is both commonsensical and intuitive. Yet, many questions about the idea are still open; there is complex discussion about whether and to what extent and under what circumstances the prices determined in a prediction market actually reflect the parameters of a probability distribution that determines the market's fundamentals that underlie the prices.

How practical is the idea of using a prediction market to evaluate the likelihood of commercialization of SBIR Phase II projects? We have focused on the winner-take-all contract, but for all of the types of contracts the same essential issues about the practicality of designing a successful prediction market must be addressed. Wolfers and Zitzewitz (2004) enumerate several key issues for the design and implementation of a successful prediction market. Key issues include the clarity of the contracts; as discussed above, the contracts for a SBIR prediction market must specify clearly the criteria for commercialization and should specify a date by which those criteria are to be met. A key condition addressed in our previous research is perhaps the most fundamental of the conditions that must be met for a prediction market to succeed—namely, in showing the relation between outside finance and commercialization, we have adduced evidence to address if a diversity of information exists in a way that provides a basis for trading (Wolfers and Zitzewitz, 2004). The other key design issues discussed by Wolfers and Zitzewitz—such as the method by which buyers are matched to sellers, the clear specification of the contracts, and whether or not real money is used—are at least relatively straightforward to address administratively.[4]

The key condition on which we focus is the need for informed traders in the market, and as the literature about prediction markets explains there must be uninformed traders as well.[5] Having uninformed traders—those trading based on relatively less reliable information or using relatively less reliable models to process the information—is at least arguably something to be expected. Possibly there will be traders who enjoy gambling on the success of R&D projects that capture their fancy,

DOI: 10.1057/9781137370884

yet are not fully understood in terms of either the technical challenges to be overcome during the Phase II R&D investment or the subsequent business challenges. The critical issue is if there would be a large number of informed traders. The findings summarized in Table 8.3 suggest that outside private investors are able to choose the right projects to support. The probability of commercialization is significantly higher for projects on which outside private investors have placed their bets, gambling that the project will pay off once commercialized.

## Employment growth from SBIR-funded projects

Although employment growth is not an explicit objective of the SBIR program, either in its original form from the 1982 Act or in its many extensions and reauthorizations, Congressional hearings in support of the 2012 reauthorization emphatically emphasized employment-related issues (Link, 2011).

We have (Link and Scott, 2012c) calculated employment growth that is directly attributable to a SBIR award—what could be termed short-run employment growth as contrasted to the long-run trajectory of the firm's employment growth that may be influenced by the SBIR award—from the NRC database. The average number of employees (*empt*) and the average number of employees retained in 2005 as a result of the technology developed during the SBIR-funded project (*retainees*) are summarized descriptively in Table 8.5, by agency.

Table 8.6 summarizes the data underlying Table 8.5 in percentage and distributional terms (and it reinforces the descriptive statistics in Table 8.1). On average, weighted by the number of projects funded by each agency, over 40 percent of all completed projects retained 0 employees, and over 33 percent retained only 1 or 2 employees. Thus, on average, the direct short-run impact of SBIR-funded projects on employment is small, especially when compared to the mean of number of employees in firms.

Although Table 8.6 shows that there are a few cases with a large number of employees retained by the firms because of their SBIR Phase II awards, clearly on average the numbers of retainees have been small. However, we found (Link and Scott, 2012a, 2012c) that the number of retainees varies systematically across agencies based on distinct project and firm characteristics.[6] When a particular explanatory variable had

DOI: 10.1057/9781137370884

TABLE 8.5 *Descriptive statistics on employees (empt) and retainees (retainees), by agency*

| Variable | n | Mean | Std. Dev. | Min. | Max. |
|---|---|---|---|---|---|
| **DoD** | | | | | |
| empt | 755 | 35.46 | 61.51 | 1 | 326 |
| retainees | 755 | 2.000 | 5.281 | 0 | 73 |
| **NIH** | | | | | |
| empt | 391 | 20.50 | 38.98 | 1 | 301 |
| retainees | 391 | 2.335 | 8.626 | 0 | 149 |
| **NASA** | | | | | |
| empt | 155 | 45.66 | 78.47 | 1 | 376 |
| retainees | 155 | 1.368 | 2.996 | 0 | 22 |
| **DOE** | | | | | |
| empt | 140 | 33.14 | 60.11 | 1 | 451 |
| retainees | 140 | 1.379 | 2.012 | 0 | 15 |
| **NSF** | | | | | |
| empt | 141 | 23.54 | 37.03 | 1 | 201 |
| retainees | 141 | 1.957 | 3.077 | 0 | 15 |

*Source*: Based on Link and Scott (2012c, p. 271).

TABLE 8.6 *Percentage of SBIR projects with firms retaining the stated number of employees after completion of Phase II project*

| Agency | n | 0 employees | 1–2 employees | 3–4 employees | 5–10 employees | >10 employees |
|---|---|---|---|---|---|---|
| DoD | 755 | 44.0 | 36.3 | 10.5 | 6.8 | 2.5 |
| NIH | 391 | 41.2 | 37.9 | 12.3 | 6.4 | 2.3 |
| NASA | 155 | 52.3 | 34.2 | 7.1 | 3.9 | 2.6 |
| DOE | 140 | 45.0 | 37.9 | 11.4 | 5.0 | 0.7 |
| NSF | 141 | 41.1 | 34.0 | 12.8 | 7.8 | 4.3 |

*Source*: Based on Link and Scott (2012a, p. 46; 2012c, p. 271).

statistically significant effects, often the direction of those effects differed across agencies. We interpret this econometric finding as support for the observation, often made, that SBIR programs in different agencies have unique characteristics.[7]

Yet, there are also many cases in which all of the statistically significant effects for an explanatory variable have the same sign for all agencies. Among such cases is the finding—supporting Nelson's (1982) observations developed from case studies—that public funding of privately performed research is more likely to lead to commercialized results and

DOI: 10.1057/9781137370884

employment gains when the government has a direct need for the products, processes, or services developed by the research projects. In such cases, the government can provide the research direction and guidance of a potential customer for the output from a research project, and it also can provide a ready market for that output. The public funding of research is therefore more likely to stimulate employment.

When exploring the range of the employees retained, we also found (Link and Scott, 2012a, 2012c) that some commercial agreement variables such as licensing agreements are associated with fewer employees retained specifically because of the SBIR project. That finding supports the belief that an important part of the employment impact of the SBIR program occurs elsewhere in the national and international economies, and we return to discussion of that possibility subsequently when we discuss the effects of the SBIR Phase II awards on the firms' long-run growth. When the recipient of a SBIR award creates new technology and then sells the rights to the technology, the SBIR program's goals of stimulating innovation and increasing commercialization have been met, and the employment effect (which is not one of the stated goals of the SBIR program) will be observed at other firms. Such spillover effects are consistent with the findings from our evaluation, reviewed in Chapter 9, of DoD SBIR projects.

Finally, university participation in a SBIR project appears to influence the level of retainees only among DoD and NIH award recipients. University participation had a positive influence on the level of retainees among DoD award recipients and a negative impact among NIH award recipients. Perhaps the role of universities is different between the types of projects undertaken by firms funded by these two agencies. Recall from Table 8.1 that only NIH projects were involved in commercializable or potentially commercializable drugs and biologics.

We (Link and Scott, 2012a, 2012b) also estimated long-run employment growth using a firm employment growth model.[8] The model was formulated so that predicted employment growth could be estimated from a growth model in which all of the explanatory variables were pre-award variables. That is, employment growth in the absence of the SBIR award was predicted on the basis of pre-award information.

Table 8.7 and Figure 8.2 show the mean actual employment (see Table 8.1) and the employment predicted, for the firm receiving a Phase II award, from the estimation of the growth model using pre-award explanatory variables. In all agencies except NSF, the mean actual growth

DOI: 10.1057/9781137370884

TABLE 8.7 *Mean actual and predicted employment for Phase II SBIR award recipients, by agency*

| Agency | n | Actual | Predicted |
|--------|------|--------|-----------|
| DoD | 755 | 59.93 | 31.38 |
| NIH | 391 | 60.41 | 19.10 |
| NASA | 155 | 62.54 | 48.71 |
| DOE | 140 | 55.71 | 34.11 |
| NSF | 141 | 40.99 | 79.16 |
| | 1,582 | | |

*Source*: Based on Link and Scott (2012a, p. 75; 2012b, p. 16).

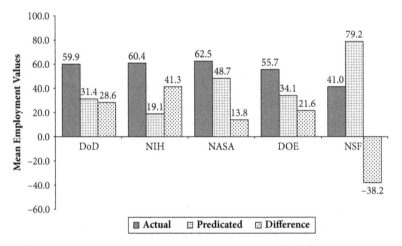

FIGURE 8.2 *Mean actual and predicted employment for Phase II SBIR award recipients, by agency*
*Source*: Prepared by the authors.

in employees calculated from the NRC data exceeded the mean predicted growth in employees. Thus, on average, there was among the NRC sample of firm projects positive firm employment growth identified as being directly attributable to the SBIR award. However, few of the measured average gains in firm employment attributable to the SBIR award were statistically significant. In fact, of the 755 DoD projects, only 10 firms had SBIR-induced employment growth that was statistically different from zero; 16 of 391 NIH-funded firms had significant SBIR-induced positive employment growth, and 1 of 155 NASA firm and 1 of 140 DOE firms also had significant positive employment growth.

DOI: 10.1057/9781137370884

Emphasizing that the SBIR-induced employment growth is the growth above and beyond what would have been predicted for the firms in the absence of the SBIR support, arguably the public support is needed for socially useful projects precisely when the odds of spectacular success are very low. The private sector would not take the risk of investing in such projects, yet by supporting a large portfolio of them the public can reap the benefits when the spectacular successes occur.

On the whole, although the economic effects of SBIR funding on overall long-run employment growth were not statistically significant, the effects are fairly large in absolute terms in Table 8.7. When the mean employment gains in Table 8.7 are denominated in terms of the dollar amount of the SBIR awards, the mean employment gains per million dollars awarded is sizeable, ranging from 24.4 employees per million dollars awarded among NASA-funded firms to 65.0 employees per million dollars awarded among NIH-funded firms.[9]

To study in more detail the SBIR-award recipient's employment growth above and beyond what would have been predicted in the counterfactual circumstances without the SBIR award—that is, the award's impact on the firm's long-run growth trajectory, or stated more boldly the bend in the firm's arc of innovation—we (Link and Scott, forthcoming) studied a large sample of firms that received DoD SBIR awards.[10]

The presence of outside funding for the Phase II project, commercial agreements with other firms, federal acquisitions, and intellectual property protection for the project's results are all expected to improve the possibility that the project will support employment growth; yet, all of those explanatory factors are likely to be influenced by the results developed from the project itself. Instead of specifying a functional form for each of these endogenous explanatory variables, we estimated the one equation, for long-run SBIR-induced employment through publicly subsidized R&D, from such a multiple-equation system, and we instrumented the endogenous explanatory variables.

For instruments, we used the variables describing prior funding (i.e., funding for the research that was obtained before the Phase II SBIR award), and we also used a set of qualitative variables for the U.S. states in which the firms receiving the SBIR awards are located. Because past experience is expected to be a good predictor of future capabilities and outcomes, a firm's prior funding might logically be correlated with the provision of outside financing for the Phase II project itself and also will be correlated with the ability to develop intellectual property and make

DOI: 10.1057/9781137370884

commercial agreements. Yet the prior funding would be predetermined rather than resulting endogenously with the evolution and success of the Phase II project after it has begun. Also, the availability of venture capital and other sources of external funding, as well as economic conditions, will vary from one state to another. Logically, then, the U.S. state qualitative variables will be correlated with other funding and intellectual property and commercial agreement capabilities, yet the variance in the qualitative indicators of the states would not be endogenously determined by the SBIR Phase II project.

We (Link and Scott, forthcoming) then used the model estimated with instrumental variables to simulate the effects for key variables in the model. We focused on the firm's net gain in long-run employment—namely the firm's gain in employment above and beyond what we estimated would be predicted for its employment in the counterfactual case where it had not received the SBIR award. First, for a typical baseline case using specified, typical settings for the variables, the net gain in employment induced by the publicly subsidized R&D is 34 percent of the employment predicted for the firm in the counterfactual case without the public subsidy of its Phase II SBIR R&D project.

Keeping all other variables at their baseline level, an increase, other things held at the baseline level, of outside finance to a standard deviation above its mean increased the net employment gain to 80 percent of the counterfactual employment. The measure of outside finance was the amount of outside finance (i.e., other than the funding provided by the SBIR program or provided by the firm itself or its principals, or provided by colleges and universities) during the Phase II project relative to total investment (including the SBIR Phase II award) in the Phase II project.[11]

Lerner and Kegler (2000), in their review of the literature about the SBIR program, explained how the firms providing outside finance help to ensure the commercial success of the small businesses with research supported by the SBIR program. Lerner and Kegler explained how venture capital organizations carefully study a firm's business plan, and if the decision is made to invest in the firm, the funds are often disbursed in stages so that the small firm must return to its source of outside financial support repeatedly allowing review of the use of the funds as the R&D project progresses. Lerner and Kegler observed that during this process, venture capitalists monitor the managers of the firm they are supporting. It is not surprising then that we find that outside financing for a firm's

SBIR project has a positive effect on the SBIR-induced employment growth of the firm.

A DoD-funded firm that has achieved manufacturing agreements using the technology created with its subsidized research, other things being at the baseline level that was for the typical case without such agreements, has an expected net gain in employment that is five times the counterfactual predicted employment.

There are statements by the principals of the firms with SBIR projects from case studies of DoD SBIR projects (Wessner, 2000) explaining that collaboration through commercial agreements with other firms helps to ensure the commercial success of the SBIR projects. For example, one entrepreneurial SBIR-supported company's founder said that he did the technical work, but that the success of his company depended importantly on his willingness to obtain outside help with the business aspects of innovation (Scott, 2000b, p. 125). This founder said, "The SBIR program could encourage small businesses to bring in outside expertise to ensure competence in business administration to go along with the competence in the scientific work." Another DoD-SBIR-supported company's founder said, when discussing Phase II of SBIR support (Scott, 2000b, p. 127):

> The prospects for commercialization could be improved if the SBIR program provided funding for a Mentor/Consultant as a part of Phase II. The SBIR firm would identify in the Phase II proposal a large corporation or marketing consulting firm that would work with the SBIR firm during Phase II and provide expertise about commercializing the technology. The small firm knows the technology, but the larger firm would act as a mentor during Phase II and would be able to help the small firm understand how to market the technology. The big company with the marketing channels and capabilities needed would look at the small company's innovative device and advise it on how to proceed.... A cross section of the mentoring company would be needed. Someone from marketing, someone from engineering, someone from administration, finance, and management.... Providing the opportunity of mentoring from and consulting with a large corporation could improve the prospects for commercialization of SBIR results.

Again, given the perceptions of small SBIR-supported firms that outside business expertise is often important for commercial success, it is not surprising that we identify positive effects on the SBIR-induced employment growth when the SBIR-supported firms have entered into commercial agreements for the use of the technologies created with their SBIR projects.

DOI: 10.1057/9781137370884

*Ceteris paribus*, the presence of R&D agreements is associated with less than predicted employment, with the shortfall being 48 percent of the predicted employment. We expect that scenario corresponds to a small firm that focuses on R&D and then sells technology to other firms rather than itself producing products using the technology. For example, the president of a very successful DoD-SBIR-award recipient firm explained that his firm was not interested in growing, saying (Archibald and Finifter, 2000, p. 225): "We remain an engineering service company that commercializes its product opportunities through licensing or the creation of separate product companies."

In this DoD sample of Phase II SBIR projects, the largest employment effect by far is for firms that have been exceptionally successful in obtaining intellectual property to protect the results of their Phase II SBIR project. *Ceteris paribus*, if the number of patents applied for based on the technology developed by a SBIR project is a standard deviation or more above the mean for the entire sample of Phase II projects, the expected value of the net employment induced by the publicly subsidized R&D is 26 times the prediction for employment in the counterfactual case without the public subsidy.[12] Thus, we see that the truly spectacular successes for publicly subsidized R&D are the cases with especially successful creation and protection of intellectual property.

Importantly, as we have emphasized, the creation and protection of intellectual property is endogenous to the evolution of the R&D projects, and for that reason the identification of its effect has required the use of instrumental variables. Also, in a separate equation, of the complete system of equations, for the endogenous explanatory variable indicating exceptional patent performance, the presence of exceptional success in creating and protecting intellectual property would be related to the endogenous explanatory variable that describes the presence of outside finance. The set of instrumental variables allows us to identify the relation between employment growth and both the intellectual property and the outside finance, but all are endogenously determined and related to one another as the publicly subsidized R&D project evolves.

We find that the employment growth from the public support of a small firm's R&D varies with the outside, third-party support for the firm and with the intellectual property created by the publicly subsidized R&D. Other things being the same, a firm with outside finance or intellectual property experiences employment growth beyond what would have been predicted for the firm in the absence of the public R&D subsidy. Commercial

DOI: 10.1057/9781137370884

agreements may be associated with employment gains for the subsidized firm, but in some cases they are also associated with lower employment growth for the small firm. We expect (and the case studies such as in Archibald and Finifter (2000, p. 225) and discussed above support this explanation) that occurs when the commercial agreements allow the small firm to earn returns on the new technology developed with the subsidized R&D, yet employment growth induced by the innovation is experienced in other firms that license the technology or purchase the rights to it.

## Relationships forged with other firms

On the basis of the NRC database, we (Link and Scott, 2012d) asked if, as a result of SBIR funding, a firm had entered into strategic commercial agreements that allowed foreign firms to exploit the technologies developed through the SBIR program and funded by U.S. taxpayers.[13]

Several generalizations can be inferred from the descriptive data in Table 8.8. One, commercial agreements by SBIR-funded firms are more common with other U.S. firms and investors than with foreign firms and investors. There are only two instances where finalized agreements with foreign firms or investors are greater than with U.S. firms or investors. Among the NASA sample, 8.0 percent of the firms had formalized a licensing agreement with foreign firms or investors compared to 6.2 percent with domestic firms or investors. And, 1.7 percent of the firms in the NSF sample had formalized a merger with foreign firms or investors compared to 0 percent with U.S. counterparts.

Two, among U.S. firms and investors, mergers and sale of the company are the least used strategies across all of the funding agencies. This compares to licensing agreements being the most used strategy by SBIR firms funded by DoD, NIH, DOE, and NSF. Following licensing agreements by firms and investors in these four agencies are R&D agreements—R&D agreements rank first among NASA firms. In addition, licensing agreements with U.S. firms and investors are at least twice as common as those with foreign firms and investors, with the exception of the NASA sample.

Three, licensing agreements and marketing/distribution agreements are the more common strategies with foreign firms or investors.

Four, R&D agreements are significantly more common with U.S. firms and investors than with foreign firms and investors. Perhaps, and this should be viewed as a tentative hypothesis, it is easier to monitor

DOI: 10.1057/9781137370884

TABLE 8.8   *Agreements with other firms or investors: percentage of the random sample of Phase II projects answering the question: "As a result of the technology developed during this project, which of the following describes your firms' activities with other firms and investors? (Select all that apply.)"*

| DoD (n = 594) | U.S. firms/investors | | Foreign firms/investors | |
|---|---|---|---|---|
| Agreement | Finalized agreements | Ongoing negotiations | Finalized agreements | Ongoing negotiations |
| Licensing agreement(s) | 15.5 | 16.5 | 2.9 | 5.2 |
| Sale of company | 1.2 | 4.9 | 0.3 | 1.0 |
| Partial sale of company | 0.8 | 4.2 | 0.0 | 1.5 |
| Sale of technology rights | 4.4 | 9.9 | 1.0 | 2.9 |
| Company merger | 0.3 | 3.2 | 0.2 | 0.7 |
| Joint venture agreement(s) | 3.7 | 8.1 | 1.2 | 2.2 |
| Marketing/distribution agreement(s) | 10.8 | 8.6 | 4.5 | 4.2 |
| Manufacturing agreement(s) | 3.4 | 8.8 | 2.7 | 2.4 |
| R&D agreement(s) | 13.8 | 13.8 | 2.5 | 3.4 |
| Customer alliance(s) | 13.1 | 14.5 | 4.2 | 3.0 |
| Other | 1.9 | 2.2 | 0.3 | 0.8 |

| NIH (n = 338) | U.S. firms/investors | | Foreign firms/investors | |
|---|---|---|---|---|
| Agreement | Finalized agreements | Ongoing negotiations | Finalized agreements | Ongoing negotiations |
| Licensing agreement(s) | 19.2 | 16.0 | 8.9 | 6.2 |
| Sale of company | 0.9 | 3.6 | 0.3 | 1.5 |
| Partial sale of company | 2.1 | 4.4 | 0.0 | 0.6 |
| Sale of technology rights | 5.6 | 7.4 | 0.6 | 0.9 |
| Company merger | 0.3 | 3.0 | 0.0 | 0.6 |
| Joint venture agreement(s) | 3.0 | 8.9 | 0.9 | 2.7 |
| Marketing/distribution agreement(s) | 21.3 | 10.4 | 12.4 | 6.5 |
| Manufacturing agreement(s) | 7.1 | 3.8 | 2.4 | 2.1 |
| R&D agreement(s) | 14.8 | 10.7 | 4.1 | 3.0 |
| Customer alliance(s) | 8.3 | 10.1 | 2.7 | 0.9 |
| Other | 2.1 | 2.1 | 0.3 | 0.9 |

*Continued*

DOI: 10.1057/9781137370884

TABLE 8.8    *Continued*

| NASA (n = 112) | U.S. firms/investors | | Foreign firms/investors | |
|---|---|---|---|---|
| Agreement | Finalized agreements | Ongoing negotiations | Finalized agreements | Ongoing negotiations |
| Licensing agreement(s) | 6.2 | 11.6 | 8.0 | 5.4 |
| Sale of company | 0.9 | 2.7 | 0.0 | 0.0 |
| Partial sale of company | 1.8 | 0.9 | 0.0 | 0.0 |
| Sale of technology rights | 0.9 | 7.1 | 0.9 | 2.7 |
| Company merger | 0.0 | 0.0 | 0.0 | 0.0 |
| Joint venture agreement(s) | 0.9 | 4.5 | 0.0 | 1.8 |
| Marketing/distribution agreement(s) | 7.1 | 5.4 | 6.2 | 1.8 |
| Manufacturing agreement(s) | 1.8 | 6.2 | 1.8 | 0.0 |
| R&D agreement(s) | 15.2 | 9.8 | 3.6 | 0.9 |
| Customer alliance(s) | 10.7 | 8.9 | 6.2 | 0.0 |
| Other | 2.7 | 3.6 | 0.9 | 0.9 |

| DOE (n = 114) | U.S. firms/investors | | Foreign firms/investors | |
|---|---|---|---|---|
| Agreement | Finalized agreements | Ongoing negotiations | Finalized agreements | Ongoing negotiations |
| Licensing agreement(s) | 15.8 | 15.8 | 5.3 | 8.8 |
| Sale of company | 0.9 | 0.9 | 0.9 | 0.9 |
| Partial sale of company | 2.6 | 1.8 | 0.0 | 1.8 |
| Sale of technology rights | 5.3 | 6.1 | 0.9 | 3.5 |
| Company merger | 0.0 | 0.9 | 0.0 | 0.9 |
| Joint venture agreement(s) | 2.6 | 7.0 | 0.0 | 2.6 |
| Marketing/distribution agreement(s) | 9.6 | 7.0 | 8.8 | 2.6 |
| Manufacturing agreement(s) | 6.1 | 6.1 | 0.9 | 4.4 |
| R&D agreement(s) | 7.9 | 10.5 | 1.8 | 6.1 |
| Customer alliance(s) | 7.9 | 13.2 | 4.4 | 5.3 |
| Other | 2.6 | 0.0 | 0.9 | 0.0 |

*Continued*

DOI: 10.1057/9781137370884

TABLE 8.8  *Continued*

| NSF (n = 121) | U.S. firms/investors | | Foreign firms/investors | |
|---|---|---|---|---|
| Agreement | Finalized agreements | Ongoing negotiations | Finalized agreements | Ongoing negotiations |
| Licensing agreement(s) | 19.8 | 21.5 | 9.9 | 6.6 |
| Sale of company | 2.5 | 3.3 | 0.0 | 0.8 |
| Partial sale of company | 2.5 | 5.8 | 1.7 | 1.7 |
| Sale of technology rights | 5.0 | 15.7 | 4.1 | 3.3 |
| Company merger | 0.0 | 4.1 | 1.7 | 0.8 |
| Joint venture agreement(s) | 3.3 | 9.9 | 0.8 | 2.5 |
| Marketing/distribution agreement(s) | 15.7 | 12.4 | 8.3 | 2.5 |
| Manufacturing agreement(s) | 8.3 | 9.9 | 3.3 | 2.5 |
| R&D agreement(s) | 17.4 | 17.4 | 5.0 | 6.6 |
| Customer alliance(s) | 11.6 | 18.2 | 3.3 | 4.1 |
| Other | 1.7 | 2.5 | 0.8 | 0.0 |

*Note*: The overall percentage of projects that have agreement activities is less than would be the case if the percentages of projects were additive across the types of categories. They are not additive. Thus, for example for DoD, it will not in general be the case that 16% of the Phase II projects have finalized U.S. licensing agreements while a completely different set of 14% have finalized U.S. R&D agreements and then yet another distinct 13% have finalized U.S. customer alliances. To determine the percentage of the random sample of Phase II projects with U.S. agreements, with foreign agreements, and with both U.S. and foreign agreements, we constructed the qualitative variables defined in the note to Table 8.9. Those variables are defined for all agencies.

*Source*: Based on Link and Scott (2012d, pp. 379–380).

information leakages that are inevitable during collaborative R&D when the partner firms or investors are geographically closer and within the same boundaries of intellectual property protection, that is, with a U.S. partner rather than a foreign partner.

As shown in Table 8.9, U.S. only agreements are more prevalent than U.S. and foreign firm or investor agreements. Foreign only agreements are the least prevalent. Thus, the data in Tables 8.8 and 8.9 provide suggestive evidence to conclude that U.S. SBIR funds for Phase II projects and the technologies associated with those projects are not, to a pronounced extent, benefiting foreign firms through agreements with SBIR firms or investors. In that sense, there is no evidence that the technologies developed with funds from U.S. taxpayers are, to any significant extent, being exploited by foreign firms through commercial agreements with SBIR-funded firms. If there were such evidence of a substantial flow

DOI: 10.1057/9781137370884

TABLE 8.9    *Descriptive statistics for the presence of agreements*

| DoD | n | Mean | Std. Dev. | Min. | Max. |
|---|---|---|---|---|---|
| U.S. agreement(s) only[a] | 594 | 0.478 | 0.500 | 0 | 1 |
| Foreign agreement(s) only[b] | 594 | 0.0522 | 0.223 | 0 | 1 |
| U.S. and foreign agreement(s)[c] | 594 | 0.143 | 0.350 | 0 | 1 |

| NIH | n | Mean | Std. Dev. | Min. | Max. |
|---|---|---|---|---|---|
| U.S. agreement(s) only | 338 | 0.441 | 0.497 | 0 | 1 |
| Foreign agreement(s) only | 338 | 0.0562 | 0.231 | 0 | 1 |
| U.S. and foreign agreement(s) | 338 | 0.237 | 0.426 | 0 | 1 |

| NASA | n | Mean | Std. Dev. | Min. | Max. |
|---|---|---|---|---|---|
| U.S. agreement(s) only | 112 | 0.366 | 0.484 | 0 | 1 |
| Foreign agreement(s) only | 112 | 0.0446 | 0.207 | 0 | 1 |
| U.S. and foreign agreement(s) | 112 | 0.179 | 0.385 | 0 | 1 |

| DOE | n | Mean | Std. Dev. | Min. | Max. |
|---|---|---|---|---|---|
| U.S. agreement(s) only | 114 | 0.395 | 0.491 | 0 | 1 |
| Foreign agreement(s) only | 114 | 0.070 | 0.257 | 0 | 1 |
| U.S. and foreign agreement(s) | 114 | 0.228 | 0.421 | 0 | 1 |

| NSF | n | Mean | Std. Dev. | Min. | Max. |
|---|---|---|---|---|---|
| U.S. agreement(s) only | 121 | 0.521 | 0.502 | 0 | 1 |
| Foreign agreement(s) only | 121 | 0.083 | 0.276 | 0 | 1 |
| U.S. and foreign agreement(s) | 121 | 0.240 | 0.429 | 0 | 1 |

*Notes*: The variable measuring agreements of any type is a 0/1 variable that equals 1 whenever any one or more of the 11 commercial agreement variables for which we have information equals 1, and is 0 otherwise. In other words, this new summary variable simply controls for the presence of some type of commercial agreement.
[a] U.S. agreement(s) only: 0/1 with 1 indicating agreement(s)—finalized or ongoing negotiations—with U.S. companies or investors only.
[b] Foreign agreement(s) only: 0/1 with 1 indicating agreement(s)—finalized or ongoing negotiations—with foreign companies or investors only.
[c] U.S. and foreign agreement(s): 0/1 with 1 indicating both U.S. and foreign agreements
*Source*: Based on Link and Scott (2012d, p. 381).

of SBIR technology to foreign firms, one could reasonably ask whether the U.S. SBIR firms captured a substantial part of the benefits from the applications of the SBIR technology by the foreign firms. But, that question need not be asked.

Finally, in Table 8.10, the use of alternative strategies is examined by observing the level of sales from the specific technology developed

DOI: 10.1057/9781137370884

TABLE 8.10 *Descriptive statistics for sales categories with and without U.S. and foreign agreements*

| DoD | n | Mean | Std. Dev. | Min. | Max. |
|---|---|---|---|---|---|
| Sales for the Phase II projects providing information about agreements | 594 | 1,763,832 | 9,659,895 | 0 | $2.01 \times 10^8$ |
| Sales with no agreements | 194 | 972,675 | 3,941,742 | 0 | $4.93 \times 10^7$ |
| Sales with U.S. agreement(s) only | 284 | 1,116,917 | 3,264,621 | 0 | $3.50 \times 10^7$ |
| Sales with foreign agreement(s) only | 31 | 1,992,457 | 6,504,660 | 0 | $3.50 \times 10^7$ |
| Sales with U.S. and foreign agreements | 85 | 5,647,607 | $2.35 \times 10^7$ | 0 | $2.01 \times 10^8$ |

| NIH | n | Mean | Std. Dev. | Min. | Min. |
|---|---|---|---|---|---|
| Sales for the Phase II projects providing information about agreements | 338 | 2,003,032 | $1.01 \times 10^7$ | 0 | $1.00 \times 10^8$ |
| Sales with no agreements | 90 | 320,273 | 800,612 | 0 | $5.00 \times 10^6$ |
| Sales with U.S. agreement(s) only | 149 | 1,061,330 | 4,849,109 | 0 | $4.00 \times 10^7$ |
| Sales with foreign agreement(s) only | 19 | 6,787,637 | $1.94 \times 10^7$ | 0 | $8.18 \times 10^7$ |
| Sales with U.S. and foreign agreements | 80 | 4,513,711 | $1.70 \times 10^7$ | 0 | $1.00 \times 10^8$ |

| NASA | n | Mean | Std. Dev. | Min. | Max. |
|---|---|---|---|---|---|
| Sales for the Phase II projects providing information about agreements | 112 | 917,510 | 2,313,071 | 0 | $1.51 \times 10^7$ |
| Sales with no agreements | 46 | 430,520 | 853,384 | 0 | $4.00 \times 10^6$ |
| Sales with U.S. agreement(s) only | 41 | 938,914 | 2,375,296 | 0 | $1.35 \times 10^7$ |
| Sales with foreign agreement(s) only | 5 | 2,616,600 | 4,518,742 | 0 | $1.06 \times 10^7$ |
| Sales with U.S. and foreign agreements | 20 | 1,568,936 | 3,402,045 | 0 | $1.51 \times 10^7$ |

| DOE | n | Mean | Std. Dev. | Min. | Max. |
|---|---|---|---|---|---|
| Sales for the Phase II projects providing information about agreements | 114 | 1,024,187 | 3,023,294 | 0 | $2.34 \times 10^7$ |
| Sales with no agreements | 35 | 286,348 | 715,591 | 0 | $3.50 \times 10^6$ |
| Sales with U.S. agreement(s) only | 45 | 1,376,243 | 4,218,549 | 0 | $2.34 \times 10^7$ |
| Sales with foreign agreement(s) only | 8 | 2,314,325 | 4,464,564 | 0 | $1.25 \times 10^7$ |
| Sales with U.S. and foreign agreements | 26 | 1,011,140 | 1,482,369 | 0 | $5.50 \times 10^6$ |

*Continued*

DOI: 10.1057/9781137370884

TABLE 8.10   *Continued*

| NSF | n | Mean | Std. Dev. | Min. | Max. |
|---|---|---|---|---|---|
| Sales for the Phase II projects providing information about agreements | 121 | 2,431,395 | $1.85 \times 10^7$ | 0 | $2.03 \times 10^8$ |
| Sales with no agreements | 19 | 210,230 | 438,816 | 0 | $1.47 \times 10^6$ |
| Sales with U.S. agreement(s) only | 63 | 3,802,841 | $2.56 \times 10^7$ | 0 | $2.03 \times 10^8$ |
| Sales with foreign agreement(s) only | 10 | 463,741 | 392,028 | 0 | $1.00 \times 10^6$ |
| Sales with U.S. and foreign agreements | 29 | 1,585,795 | 3,478,123 | 0 | $1.79 \times 10^7$ |

*Source*: Based on Link and Scott (2012d, p. 382).

during the Phase II project. Regardless of funding agency, the mean sales (by 2005) for those projects with no agreements—U.S. or foreign agreement—are less than for projects with agreements. And, mean sales are greater when there are agreements with foreign firms or investors than when there are only U.S. agreements. This finding, albeit based only on descriptive evidence and in some cases descriptive evidence based only on a handful of observations, suggests that when such technology transfer does occur through commercial agreements among SBIR firms and foreign firms and investors, it is with projects that are relatively more successful as measured in terms of cumulative sales, supporting the belief that, for those cases, the SBIR firms are reaping substantial benefits from the technologies developed with the funds from U.S. taxpayers.

## In their own words

In the discussions of the econometric findings about the importance for commercial success of outside finance and collaborations with other firms, we have quoted the observations of the principals in several firms receiving SBIR awards. We conclude this section with additional observations from the recipients of SBIR awards about the SBIR program that has supported their research.

In the observations quoted earlier, the award recipients supported the encouragement of cooperation with other firms to provide outside expertise in taking the technology produced with a SBIR award and successfully commercializing it. Award recipients recognized that they—the small firm doing the research supported by the SBIR

DOI: 10.1057/9781137370884

program—may not have the necessary expertise in manufacturing and marketing to translate the technology into a commercial success. The combination of the econometric findings about the importance of outside private finance and collaborations with other firms, along with the observations we have quoted, support consideration of a policy recommendation that as a part of a firm's application for Phase II SBIR support the firm would also seek outside third-party support in the form of both outside finance and cooperative agreements with larger firms that might provide appropriate expertise in the commercialization of technology developed with the Phase II award. Possibly, as with the DoD's fast-track program that gave higher priority to funding proposals with outside finance already in place, the firms that are successful in achieving outside partnerships for their projects could get priority for the evaluation of their proposals.

Yet requiring such collaborative relationships or even formal partnerships as a prerequisite for successful applications for Phase II SBIR support could be viewed as too rigid a policy requirement. Some socially desirable projects would have little chance of achieving outside private support until after the public support was in place. As illustrated and discussed in Chapter 2, public support through the SBIR program increases the expected private rate of return and lowers the downside risk of a project. Thus, it might be more appropriate to have a requirement for a contingent commitment, whereby the outside partner would commit to providing outside support contingent on SBIR Phase II support.

To conclude this section about the NRC-sponsored studies, we offer more observations from the principals at selected firms that received SBIR awards.[14] In answer to the question of whether the company would have undertaken the SBIR-supported research without the SBIR award, the following representative comments are paraphrased from the interviews with the award recipients. Many of the comments make clear that any new requirement about outside support for finance or business expertise should be flexible, perhaps using the idea of a contingent commitment from the outside organization providing the support. The comments also reinforce the econometric evidence we have adduced about risk and about long-run trajectory for firm growth; the comments provide anecdotal evidence about risk in terms of the probability of commercialization of the technology created with a SBIR Phase II award, and also about how it is that a SBIR Phase II

DOI: 10.1057/9781137370884

award can change a small company's trajectory of growth. Here now are some of the interview comments in response to the question: Would your company have undertaken the research without the SBIR award?[15]

> No. To support our Phase I project, we tried to find support from other companies and venture capitalists. The venture capitalists want too high a rate of return and want returns too quickly. Joint ventures don't work either. You need the money, so they want lots of rights. You must sell your soul to them. These partner companies are providing capital basically and sometimes distribution networks.

> No. Working on a particular DoD program enabled us to do further work on our technology and gain insight into commercialization. The SBIR project is an incubation period of sorts to new start-up companies with new technology, an innovative way of approaching a problem. After the SBIR project, the development work that remains is a reorientation of the technology, looking at how to manufacture and commercialize for nonmilitary applications, to come up with a low-cost way to mass produce for less sophisticated requirements. But at the outset, the SBIR award is the lifeblood of new entrepreneurial ventures when new technology is to be advanced. We came up with something worthwhile for DoD, but we also advanced our own technology to another level without going crazy looking for outside investors. The lessons learned in the SBIR project provide the database that allows us to extrapolate intelligently and succeed in nonmilitary, commercial applications of our technology.

> We would have devoted some resources to the project, but it is questionable whether we would have gotten this far [with our research]. We would have sought assistance from other companies and from universities. We would have proceeded on a smaller scale and sought a partner down the road.

> No. There is no guarantee that such high-risk research will pan out. And the SBIR program understands that, and it therefore requires not necessarily a commercial product, but instead a good effort. It understands that in many cases the value will be to prove the technological approach taken is *not* the right path. So the [funding agency within DoD] will not go down that path again. In fact, in the case of our award, [the funding agency] gave two awards. So, it spends $1.5 million on two projects running parallel, and the probability of at least one success is increased. We'll have a cookoff... with the other company to see which box is the better to go with.

DOI: 10.1057/9781137370884

Probably not. We have no means of acquiring capital except through loans or from investors. But being honest with them, we could not raise the necessary funds—at least not at the outset of the SBIR projects. DoD does not select its highest priority acquisition projects to develop through the SBIR program. Instead, it uses projects that are interesting and have great potential value and the possibility for acquisition. But they are lower priority, high-risk projects. It is difficult to attract outside investment for such projects. These are projects for which we could not show an outside investor definite acquisition plans. If we could, DoD would not use the SBIR program to fund the projects. The SBIR projects are ones for which the acquisition plans are fuzzy.

No. We would not have done the project without the SBIR award....Without SBIR help, our research would have been more near-term and less challenging.

...after we had used Phase I for risk reduction, we became convinced that the technology would work, but then only after [completion of Phase II when] we had a patent were we willing to approach the large companies for a partnership. A small business [like ours] needs to have a patent in hand in our area of technology. The big companies, in our area, will say: "We do not sign nondisclosure agreements with small companies."

To conclude this section of statements of the principals at firms that have received SBIR awards, we add a few interview responses to the questions: Do you anticipate applying for SBIR awards in the future? Why?

Yes. It's the only way to keep the lights on, given the high risk and high capital costs for the research we are doing as we try to get into a different technology. Our existing line of business generates very little revenue and we cannot fund R&D ourselves. For the type of research we are doing, neither venture capitalists nor large companies will work as sources of outside funding. Both the venture capitalists and the large companies want too high a rate of return—too many rights to the future returns relative to the investment they would make in our company.

Yes. The SBIR program is the way to get funds for truly innovative high-risk small business projects that cannot effectively be financed by outside private funds, given the opportunistic behavior by companies or lack of understanding of the technology by venture capitalists.

Yes. The SBIR awards help us research new technologies, given technical risk and the risk of opportunistic behavior by large companies if we go to them with our ideas before they are developed.

Yes. SBIR awards let us accept the risk of good projects.

DOI: 10.1057/9781137370884

# Notes

1   However, it is important to point out that the NRC survey was not sufficiently robust to determine if the newly hired employees were the ones retained, or if other employees were retained as a result of complementarities between the funded research and other technology development efforts within the firm.

2   Zeckhauser (1996, p. 12746) was subtle when he referred to the supposed importance of industry-supported research to universities as he describes how such relationships might develop: "Information gifts [to industry] may be a part of [a university's] commercial courtship ritual."

3   The remainder of this chapter draws from Link and Scott (2009).

4   In the context of a SBIR prediction market, Zitzewitz noted (personal correspondence, December 11, 2006) there are special questions to address: "One would have to give some thought into how much information about the new technologies firms would disclose, and to whom the market would be open. This may especially be an issue for DoD projects (i.e., would they need to be U.S. citizens, require clearances, etc.)".

5   See especially the discussion in Wolfers and Zitzewitz (2006), as well as the discussion in Wolfers and Zitzewitz (2004).

6   This finding could be inferred from the descriptive statistics in Table 5.

7   See the quoted passage above from Wessner (2008).

8   Our model was of the form:

$$y(t) = a \, e^{gt} \, e^{\varepsilon} \tag{1}$$

where $y(t)$ is the number of employees $t$ years after the firm was founded; $a$ is the start-up number of employees; $g$ is the annual rate of growth of employees (estimated with pre-award data and then used as the rate for our counterfactual prediction of growth after the firm received a SBIR Phase II award); and $\varepsilon$ is a random error term. The growth of employment is assumed to be a function of explanatory variables $x$, though $x_k$ as:

$$(\partial y(t) / \partial t) / y(t) = g = b_0 + b_1 x_1 + \ldots + b_k x_k \tag{2}$$

From equation (1) it follows that:

$$\ln y(t) = \ln a + gt + \varepsilon \tag{3}$$

Substituting $g$ in equation (2) into equation (3) yields:

$$\ln y(t) = \ln a + b_0 t + b_1 x_1 t + \ldots + b_k x_k t + \varepsilon \tag{4}$$

where the explanatory variables are defined from pre-award variables in the NRC database so that $\ln y(t)$ can be predicted under the counterfactual assumption that the firm did not receive a SBIR award.

9   See Link and Scott (2012a, p. 76).

DOI: 10.1057/9781137370884

10 This subsection draws from Link and Scott (forthcoming). We focused on the DoD sample because it was by far the largest sample, and a large sample was especially desirable because we used an instrumental variables estimator.

11 The outside financing variable does not include the funding from colleges and universities; funding from those sources was controlled separately because funding from academia is arguably more analogous to direct research support rather than being simply generic funding for the operation of the project.

12 The average number of patent applications for our sample of 562 completed DoD-SBIR Phase II projects was 1.1 with a range from 0 to 100. There were 15 cases for which the dichotomous patent variable here was equal to 1, and for those 15 cases, the average number of applications was 20.4 with a range from 6 to 100.

13 This subsection draws from Link and Scott (2012d).

14 The remainder of this section draws from Scott (2000b).

15 See Table 8.2 for a comparison of these interview quotes and responses in the NRC database.

DOI: 10.1057/9781137370884

# 9

# Toward an Evaluation of the SBIR Program

**Abstract:** *As with any public-sector program, arguments about public accountability stress the importance of demonstrating net social benefits. The extant literature on this subject is summarized in this chapter.*

Link, Albert N. and Scott, John T. (2013).
*Bending the Arc of Innovation: Public Support of R&D in Small, Entrepreneurial Firms,*
New York: Palgrave Macmillan, 2013.
DOI: 10.1057/9781137370884.

DOI: 10.1057/9781137370884

It is important to distinguish between program assessment and program evaluation. Although many use the terms interchangeably with reference to public-sector activity, a distinction is warranted. Program assessment is based primarily on the criterion of effectiveness: Has the program met its stated goals and objectives; have its designated outputs been achieved? Program evaluation is based on the criterion of efficiency: How do the social benefits associated with the program compare to the social costs? Critical to the choice of a program evaluation method is how the organization/agency is involved in the conduct of the program. Is the program, or is the program's project(s), publicly funded and publicly performed, or is it publicly funded and privately performed?

Regarding an assessment of the SBIR program, one might view our (Link and Scott, 2009, 2010) analysis of the probability of commercialization from a SBIR award as a partial assessment of the program. Recall that a stated objective of the program in the 1982 Act was: "(4) to increase private sector commercialization of innovations derived from Federal research and development."

We use the phrase *partial assessment* because the NRC database does not contain information on projects not funded through the SBIR program, regardless of the agency. Thus, a matched-pairs analysis is not possible using the NRC database. If it were, one could compare the propensity to commercialize from funded and non-funded projects.

An evaluation of the entire SBIR program has yet to be conducted, although we (Link and Scott, 2000) did provide a methodology for, as well as an evaluation of, the DoD SBIR program. One can only wonder whether, if an evaluation of the entire SBIR program had been conducted to demonstrate the net social benefits attributable to the set-aside funds used for the program, the program would have been reauthorized in 2008 rather than repeatedly being temporarily reauthorized for short periods of time until the end of 2011.

The importance of program evaluation in general traces directly to the Government Performance and Results Act (GPRA) of 1993.[1] The 103rd Congress stated in the August 3, 1993 GPRA legislation that it found, based on over a year of committee study, that:

1   Waste and inefficiency in Federal programs undermine the
    confidence of the American people in the Government and
    reduce the Federal Government's ability to address adequately vital
    public needs;

DOI: 10.1057/9781137370884

2   Federal managers are seriously disadvantaged in their efforts
    to improve program efficiency and effectiveness, because of
    insufficient articulation of program goals and inadequate
    information on program performance; and
3   Congressional policymaking, spending decisions and program
    oversight are seriously handicapped by insufficient attention to
    program performance and results.

Accordingly, Congress stated the purposes of GPRA are to:

1   Improve the confidence of the American people in the capability
    of the Federal Government, by systematically holding Federal
    agencies accountable for achieving program results;
2   Initiate program performance reform with a series of pilot projects
    in setting program goals, measuring program performance against
    those goals, and reporting publicly on their progress;
3   Improve Federal program effectiveness and public accountability
    by promoting a new focus on results, service quality, and customer
    satisfaction;
4   Help Federal managers improve service delivery, by requiring that
    they plan for meeting program objectives and by providing them
    with information about program results and service quality;
5   Improve Congressional decision making by providing more objective
    information on achieving statutory objectives, and on the relative
    effectiveness and efficiency of Federal programs and spending; and
6   Improve internal management of the Federal Government.

GPRA requires that the head of each agency to:

> [P]repare an annual performance plan [beginning with fiscal year 1999]
> covering each program activity set forth in the budget of such agency. Such
> plan shall...establish performance indicators to be used in measuring or
> assessing the relevant outputs, service levels, and outcomes of each program
> activity....

And, where "performance indicators" means a particular value or char-
acteristic used to measure output or outcome.[2]

Recently, there has been a renewed public interest in program evaluation. On October 7, 2009, Peter Orszag, then Director of the Office of
Management and Budget (OMB), sent a memorandum to the heads of
executive departments and agencies on the subject of increased emphasis
on program evaluations. Therein he wrote:[3]

DOI: 10.1057/9781137370884

Rigorous, independent program evaluations can be a key resource in determining whether government programs are achieving their intended outcomes.... Evaluations can help policymakers and agency managers strengthen the design and operation of programs. Ultimately, evaluations can help the [Obama] Administration determine how to spend taxpayer dollars effectively and efficiently....

As we (Link and Scott, 2011) have argued, an appropriate method for evaluating a publicly funded, privately performed project—a SBIR-funded R&D project for example—is the Spillover Evaluation Method. The question asked in the spillover method is one that facilitates an economic understanding of whether the public sector should be under-writing the private-sector firm's activity, namely: *What is the social rate of return from the program (including spillovers) compared to the private rate of return?* Or: What proportion of the total profit stream generated by the private firm's investments does the private firm expect to capture; and hence, what proportion is not appropriated but is instead captured by other firms that imitate or use knowledge generated by the initial invest-ments to produce competing products for the social good? The part of the stream of expected profits captured by the initial investor is its private return, while the entire stream is the lower bound on the social return. In essence, this method weighs the private return, estimated through extensive interviews with firms receiving public support regarding their expectations of future patterns of events and future abilities to appropri-ate investment-based knowledge, against private investments. The social rate of return weighs the social returns against the social investments.

The application of the spillover model to an evaluation of the SBIR program is appropriate because the output of the funded project is only partially appropriable by the private firm, with the rest spilling over to society. The extent of the spillover of such knowledge with public good characteristics determines whether or not the public sector should fund the project.

We (Link and Scott, 2000) interviewed DoD-SBIR award recipients for 44 projects in 43 companies in an evaluation study that illustrates the Spillover Evaluation Method.[4] For illustrative purposes, some of these projects are described in Appendix B. Each SBIR award recipient was interviewed near the end of the Phase II award period. We collected information that allowed us to calculate a lower-bound for each project's expected social rate of return, and we then compared that expected social rate of return to both the expected private rate of return if the firm had done the project without the SBIR support and the expected private rate of return with that support. The analysis clearly indicates that, without the SBIR funding, the SBIR projects studied were like project A in Figure 2.1, but that given the SBIR funding, the projects became analogous to Figure 2.1's project B.

Table 9.1 lists the variables used to implement the Spillover Evaluation Method. The table distinguishes those data that were available from DoD project files and those data collected in the interviews. The data from DoD project files were verified during the interview process and corrected when discrepancies were found. Table 9.2 provides descriptive statistics for the variables to illustrate for the projects studied that the publicly funded and privately performed (i.e., SBIR funded) research results spill over to society—that is, to illustrate that SBIR research results are not fully appropriable by the funded firm.

Our (Link and Scott, 2000; Audretsch, Link, and Scott, 2002) evaluation of the 44 SBIR-sponsored projects showed that the expected private rate of return in the absence of SBIR support is 25 percent, clearly less than the average self-reported hurdle rate of 33 percent shown in Table 9.1. Thus, in the absence of SBIR support the sample of firms would not have undertaken the research, and in fact each of the sampled firms

TABLE 9.1    *Variables for the expected social rate of return calculations*

| Variable | Definition | Source |
|---|---|---|
| $d$ | duration of the SBIR project | DoD files, verified and updated as necessary during interviews |
| $C$ | total cost of the SBIR project | DoD files, verified and updated as necessary during interviews |
| $A$ | SBIR funding | DoD files, verified and updated as necessary during interviews |
| $r$ | private hurdle rate | interview |
| $z$ | duration of the extra period of development beyond Phase II | interview |
| $F$ | additional cost for the extra period of development | interview |
| $T$ | life of the commercialized technology | interview |
| $v$ | proportion of value appropriated | interview |
| $L$ | lower bound for expected annual private return to the SBIR firm | derived |
| $U$ | upper bound for expected annual private return to the SBIR firm | derived |

*Source*: Based on Link and Scott (2000, p. 283); Audretsch, Link, and Scott (2002, p. 154).

DOI: 10.1057/9781137370884

TABLE 9.2   *Descriptive statistics used in the social rate of return model (n = 44)*

| Variable | Mean | Std. Dev. |
|---|---|---|
| $d$ | 2.68 years | 0.36 |
| $C$ | $1,027,199 | 461,901 |
| $A$ | $782,000 | 127,371 |
| $r$ | 0.33[a] | 0.08 |
| $z$ | 1.30 years | 1.07 |
| $F$ | $1,377,341 | 2,972,266 |
| $T$ | 10.56 years | 7.23 |
| $v$ | 0.16 | 0.16 |
| $L$ | $902,738 | 1,228,850 |
| $U$ | $1,893,001 | 1,733,581 |

[a] Eight of the respondents were uncomfortable estimating the private hurdle rate that would apply to their projects at their outset. For those, the average value of $r$ for the respondents in their region was used in the calculations.
*Source*: Based on Link and Scott (2000, p. 286); Audretsch, Link, and Scott (2002, p. 154).

stated during our interviews that without the SBIR support, they would not have done the research. Further, our approximation of the lower bound for the expected social rate of return with the SBIR funding of the projects averaged 84 percent for the 44 projects; hence the projects were expected to be socially valuable.

Although we did not conclude that a social rate of return of at least 84 percent is better or worse than expected or is good or bad, we can compare the estimate to the opportunity cost of public funds promulgated by the U.S. Office of Management and Budget (OMB). Following the guidelines set forth by OMB (1992) mandating a real discount rate of 7 percent for constant-dollar benefit-to-cost analyses of proposed investments and regulations, clearly a nominal social rate of return of 84 percent is above that rate and reflects projects that are socially worthwhile in terms of the OMB standard.[5]

Figure 9.1 reprises Figure 2.1 but includes the averages for the 44 projects of the private rate of return, the private hurdle rate, and the lower bound of the social rate of return as calculated using the Spillover Evaluation Method.[6] Based on the sample of 44 projects, the average gap between the lower-bound social rate of return and the estimated private rate of return without SBIR funding support is 59 percent.

We now return to the diversity goal of the SBIR program.[7] Chapter 5 explained that in addition to the goals of stimulating technological innovation, using small business to meet Federal R&D needs, and increasing

DOI: 10.1057/9781137370884

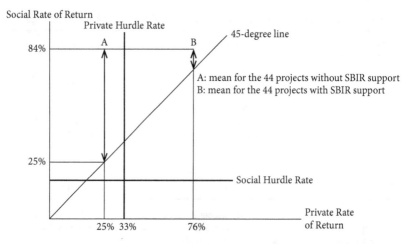

FIGURE 9.1    *Gap between social and private rates of return: average for SBIR projects, n = 44*

Source:  Based on Link and Scott (2000, p. 287); Audretsch, Link, and Scott (2002, p. 156).

private-sector commercialization of innovations derived from Federal R&D, the SBIR program has the goal of fostering and encouraging participation, in the process of technological innovation, of minority and disadvantaged persons and small businesses with majority ownership and control by women.

We conclude this section about the evaluation of the SBIR program with discussion of evidence about the redirection of R&D activity keeping in mind the goal of stimulating diversity in the process of creating and introducing technological innovations.

Scott (2000a) used NRC data about the SBIR program to illustrate the redirection of R&D activity by means of the government financing of privately performed R&D. Early in 1999, the NRC directed a study of the SBIR projects sponsored by DoD. As a part of that study, a large sample of DoD-SBIR projects was surveyed to gather information about the sponsored projects and the small businesses performing the projects. Among other things, the information collected identified projects for which the small businesses performing the research were able, early in their research projects, to secure substantial amounts of outside private financing from either venture capitalists or other companies.[8]

DOI: 10.1057/9781137370884

In 1996, DoD began its Fast Track Program that encouraged firms to find substantial outside financing early in their research projects. Obtaining such funds to combine with the government's funding qualified the project for the "fast track" of a high priority for the more substantial second stage SBIR funding that followed the initial relatively low-budget research in the first stage of the project. Firms that had previous SBIR awards were required to find more outside financing (to qualify their projects for Fast Track status) than required of firms new to the program.

The information gathered in the NRC survey to assess the DoD Fast Track Program, when combined with other information in the SBIR project files of DoD, strongly suggested that the government R&D supports projects and firms that are different from those the private sector chooses to support. The government provided support for all of the projects in the sample; the private sector provided outside, third-party support for just a subset of the projects. The private sector was much less likely to provide outside finance early in the research projects—even with the government picking up a large portion of the R&D bill—for certain types of technologies and certain types of firms.

Scott (2000a) estimated the probability of a firm obtaining early outside financing that would qualify it for Fast Track status. The probability of obtaining such outside funding increased if the firm was funded by an individual who had a business background, and if the firm was not minority owned.

Of central importance for an assessment of the SBIR diversity goal, the minority-ownership effect is large (in both a statistical sense and in magnitude). For example, other things being the same, a minority-owned firm would have a 10 to 20 percent probability of obtaining early outside finance when for a non-minority-owned firm the probability would have been 50 percent. In the circumstances of the SBIR program, this suggests that third-party financiers consider minority-ownership, other observable characteristics of the firm and its project being the same, when making investment decisions.

As discussed above, with reference to project A in Figure 2.1, SBIR is viewed as funding those projects for which there is a positive spillover gap (meaning that the social rate of return is greater than the private rate of return) and for which the private return is less than the private hurdle rate. As just discussed, there is also evidence that the SBIR program is

DOI: 10.1057/9781137370884

supporting inexperienced businesses (firms with founders without business backgrounds) and firms that are minority-owned. Thus, we have a favorable assessment of the goal of diversity to go with our favorable evaluation based on samples of DoD-funded SBIR projects.

The diversity goal has, on close examination, an interesting connection to the efficiency arguments that underlie evaluation of the SBIR program. We have seen with the Spillover Evaluation Method that the social rates of return for the SBIR projects evaluated were substantial (see Figure 7.1), and, moreover, exceeded the private rates of return in the absence of the SBIR support. Those private rates of return, however, fell short of the private hurdle rates, and consequently the research projects would not have been done without the SBIR support to bring the private rates of return above the hurdle rates.

Observe that the evaluation metrics are based on market valuations, and those valuations of course depend on the current distribution of income and hence on whose tastes count for determining market values. By addressing the diversity goal as mandated by the legislation authorizing the SBIR program, the SBIR program will perhaps have an impact on the distribution of income, changing whose tastes count in the process of casting monetary "votes" that determine the market valuations used for evaluation metrics.

The evaluation evidence shows that through the SBIR program the public sector is supporting socially desirable R&D projects that would not otherwise have been undertaken. The evidence about the probability of outside financial support for the projects is consistent with the view that, contrasted with what the private sector would do without the program, the SBIR program redirects R&D effort toward different types of technologies and redirects the performance of the R&D toward different types of firms. The SBIR program appears to bring into the innovation process firms and projects that the private sector would not have supported without the program. The program shifts resources toward firms with founders who do not have business backgrounds and toward firms that are minority-owned, toward certain types of technologies that would not have been supported by outside finance. With the new participants in the innovation process and with the new directions for the research, the distribution of the rewards of the innovation process may well change, and with the new distribution there may be a different set of market valuations that underlie evaluation. In that sense, even the

DOI: 10.1057/9781137370884

diversity goal of the SBIR program is related to the efficiency of R&D performance.

# Notes

1  The following part of this chapter, up to the presentation of our illustration of the Spillover Evaluation Method, draws from Link and Scott (2011).

2  Outputs are generally evaluated as part of an assessment, and outcomes are generally evaluated as part of an evaluation.

3  Noteworthy in the quoted passage is the juxtaposition of the words "evaluation," "outcomes," and "efficiently."

4  The following part of this section, with the illustration of the Spillover Evaluation Method, draws from Audretsch, Link, and Scott (2002) and Link and Scott (2000).

5  Link and Scott (2011) provide a detailed discussion of the OMB directive for the real discount rate of 7 percent as the social hurdle rate for public investment projects.

6  In some circumstances, expanding the questions about the spillovers can allow the spillover rate to account for approximations of the value consumers will enjoy above what they pay for the goods embodying the R&D results from the SBIR project. Link and Scott (2012f) provide an example. However, the approach taken in Link and Scott (2000) is a more conservative approach that does not attempt to approximate the spillover of value to consumer surplus.

7  The remainder of this section draws from Scott (2000a).

8  These projects are known as "Fast Track" projects, for which the performing companies obtained outside finance early, in particular, before Phase II of the project was funded.

DOI: 10.1057/9781137370884

# 10

# Concluding Observations about Public Support of R&D in Small, Entrepreneurial Firms

**Abstract:** *This chapter summarizes the earlier chapters in the monograph. Key arguments for and empirical evidence about the SBIR program are presented.*

Link, Albert N. and Scott, John T. (2013).
*Bending the Arc of Innovation: Public Support of R&D in Small, Entrepreneurial Firms,*
New York: Palgrave Macmillan, 2013.
DOI: 10.1057/9781137370884.

DOI: 10.1057/9781137370884

Based on our evaluation, summarized in Chapter 9, of a sample of DoD SBIR projects, the social returns to SBIR projects are expected to be quite high, and moreover, the projects appear to be the type of projects that require public support if the investments are to be made and their social benefits realized.

The SBIR program appears to provide benefits despite—indeed, perhaps because of—the high risk of the projects. As reviewed in Chapter 8, across the SBIR projects of DoD, NIH, NASA, DOE, and NSF, somewhat less than 50 percent of the projects achieve commercialization of their technologies. Further, and also reviewed in Chapter 8, on the dimension of employment created, very few firms with SBIR support experience success beyond what would have been predicted for them in the absence of the SBIR award. As explained in Chapters 2 and 6, the high risk underlies the market failure that can be overcome with the support of the SBIR program, allowing the private performance of R&D projects and the realization of their social benefits when those projects would not have been done without the public support.

Yet our assessment of commercialization supports the belief that perhaps the program could be better designed. As reviewed in Chapter 8, the estimated commercialization probabilities, as a function of the characteristics of the projects, show that the probability of commercialization ranges from essentially 0.0 to essentially 1.0. The range in the estimated probabilities supports the belief that it may be possible to do a better job of identifying projects with no hope of producing commercialized results and then assessing whether, despite the expectation that the SBIR's commercialization goal would not be met, the knowledge created by the project would justify supporting it because it would help meet the SBIR goal of stimulating innovation through the spillovers of the knowledge created by the publicly supported research. Projects that are predicted to be "sure bets" for commercialization could be examined especially closely to ensure that the projects are not like project B in Figure 2.1—that is, to ensure that the projects, although socially useful and having positive spillovers, are not also ones that would be undertaken without public support. Chapter 8 explains that the probability of commercial success for SBIR projects typically increases with the amount of funding provided by other sources of outside finance beyond the SBIR program. That fact is potentially useful for predicting the quality of proposed SBIR projects and for designing policy that would improve

DOI: 10.1057/9781137370884

the SBIR projects' prospects for meeting the commercialization goal of the SBIR program. Award recipients could be encouraged to obtain outside third-party support to obtain the mentoring of experienced private-sector firms. Also, possibly, prediction markets could be used to improve the probability of commercial success for projects chosen to receive SBIR support.

Chapter 8 also details the agreements that the firms receiving SBIR awards have forged with other firms. We show (Link and Scott, 2012a) that in the presence of such agreements, for example an agreement to sell to another firm the rights to the technology generated by the SBIR award, employment is sometimes less than it is at the SBIR award-recipient firms that do not have such agreements but are otherwise the same. We argue that it is then reasonable to assume that the firms using the SBIR technologies under commercial agreements will experience a positive employment impact. As reviewed in Chapter 8, whether measured as project-specific retention of employees or as overall employment growth in the SBIR firms, the impact of the SBIR awards is on average small or not statistically significant. Yet when the recipient of a SBIR award creates new technology and then sells the rights, it has certainly met the SBIR program's goals of stimulating innovation and increasing commercialization of the results of the publicly funded research. Further, the employment impact, while not a stated goal of the SBIR program, may well occur at other firms. We expect that through commercial agreements such as the sale of technology rights to other firms, the accomplishments of the innovative, entrepreneurial firms receiving SBIR awards will have socially beneficial effects for other firms and for their customers in the U.S. economy and in foreign markets.

In Chapter 8 we also explained the information gained from estimating an instrumental variables model of the firm's long-run employment growth stimulated by a SBIR award—that is, the employment growth above and beyond what is predicted for the small, entrepreneurial firm in the absence of the SBIR support. The estimation of the instrumental variables model bolsters and strengthens our inferences based on the descriptive relations showing that commercial success is more likely when the small, entrepreneurial firms supplement the SBIR awards with outside private support.

Taken together, the findings summarized in Chapter 8 suggest several interpretative points.[1]

DOI: 10.1057/9781137370884

Our findings complement the literature about the determinants of cooperation by exploring the effects of cooperation in the particular context of collaboration between outside firms and small businesses to help commercialize the publicly supported research of the small businesses. Our analysis of the effects provides understanding about the causes.

Our results support the inference that cooperating firms can better appropriate the value of knowledge spillovers than non-cooperating firms. A contractual commercial agreement between another firm and a small firm with a SBIR-award can allow more effective transfer of knowledge created with the small firm's publicly supported research because both parties to the agreement have better access to the knowledge resources of the other. The agreements allow the dedication of resources and organizational efforts necessary for the commercially successful access to and use of external knowledge.

Both the presence of outside financial support beyond the public support and the presence of commercial agreements are arguably reliable signals of the quality of the technological knowledge generated and the potential commercial success of the small firms with publicly supported R&D projects. The small firms with good research projects attract more attention from outside investors and from incumbents expecting to realize benefits from the knowledge generated by the research.

Our findings suggest that the search for cooperating partners and outside investors (and perhaps the achievement of a commitment, contingent on the forthcoming public support for the project, for the outside cooperation) might be a useful condition for the provision of public support once the small business research has proceeded beyond the initial stage Phase I award that establishes the potential and feasibility of the research and has reached Phase II when the technology will be developed to achieve its commercial potential.

In conclusion, we have suggested a few possibilities for fine-tuning the SBIR program to enhance the probability that funded projects succeed. Yet, we emphasize that the evidence, from assessments and evaluations, supports the belief that the U.S. SBIR program meets its legislated goals of stimulating technological innovation, using small business to meet Federal R&D needs, encouraging diversity among the participants in technological innovation, and increasing private-sector commercialization of technologies created with Federal R&D.

DOI: 10.1057/9781137370884

# Note

1   We are indebted to Cristiano Antonelli for his thoughts that resulted in the following interpretations that are based on the discussion in Link and Scott (forthcoming).

DOI: 10.1057/9781137370884

# Appendices

*Examples of Phase II SBIR projects*

| Funded company | Project description |
|---|---|
| *SA Photonics* | In 2010, DoD awarded $499,982 to SA Photonics, a California-based company, for a project titled "Analog to Information (A2I) Sensing for Software Defined Receivers." |
| | Compressive sensing is based on the notion that the information content of a signal may be much less than its instantaneous bandwidth, and that this signal "sparseness" can be exploited directly during the sensing operation. When applied to the sampling of pulsed radar signals, compressive sensing can allow radar signals to be sampled below (possibly well below) the Nyquist rate, allowing for a very small yet flexible software-defined Radar Warning Receiver (RWR). This compressive based RWR can detect and parameterize unknown received radar signals over the frequency range of 0.1–20 GHz and can provide parameter estimation of the received power, carrier frequency, PRF, and pulse width. With this information, available bandwidth can be determined. In this Phase II we will develop a prototype compressive-based RWR in order to validate its performance against simulated radar signals. |

*Continued*

**APPENDIX A**    *Continued*

| | |
|---|---|
| *Edvotek, Inc.* | In 2009, NIH awarded $518,708 to Edvotek, Inc., a Maryland-based company, for a project titled "Science Education of Alcohol Metabolism." |
| | Human consumption of alcohol is ubiquitous. While it is reported that 90% of the population consumes various amounts of alcohol, only a small but sizable minority of the population abuse alcohol consumption. It is estimated that 10–20% of males and 3–10% of females develop persistent alcohol-related problems. Alcohol use by youth continues to be an important health focus for our nation. Alcohol misuse among adolescents is on the increase, and excessive drinking is associated with psychological, social and physical harm to the individual, family and society. During the Phase II award period, the company researched and tested new experiments and reagents in workshop and classroom settings prior to the marketing experiments for grades 7 to 12 on understanding how alcohol is metabolized and that there are differences in the rate of metabolism amongst individuals. |
| *Spectra Research, Inc.* | In 2009, NASA awarded $599,996, a Phase II project, to Spectra Research, Inc., an Ohio-based company, for a project titled, "Dual Polarization Multi-Frequency Antenna Array." |
| | NASA employs various passive microwave and millimeter-wave instruments, such as spectral radiometers, for a wide range of remote sensing applications from measurements of the Earth's surface and atmosphere to cosmic background emission. These instruments, such as the HIRAD (Hurricane Intensity Radiometer), SFMR (Stepped Frequency Microwave Radiometer), and LRR (Lightweight Rainfall Radiometer), provide unique data accumulation capabilities for observing sea-surface wind, temperature, and rainfall and significantly enhance the understanding and predictability of hurricane intensity. These microwave instruments require extremely efficient wideband or multiband antennas. For the Phase I SBIR program, Spectra Research, Inc. teamed with Scientists from the Georgia Tech Research Institute (GTRI) to apply new technological antenna advances and new antenna design tools toward solving the challenge of designing small, multi-function antennas that reduce the space, weight, and drag demand on the platform. |
| *APS Technology, Inc.* | In 2003, DOE awarded $749,845 to APS Technology, Inc., a Connecticut-based company, for a project titled, "Rotary Steerable Motor System for Deep Gas Drilling." |
| | This project will develop a new drilling tool that allows greater power to be delivered to the drill bit while allowing the drill bit to be continuously oriented in the desired direction, thereby eliminating "crooked" holes which cause drilling, completion, and production problems. |

*Continued*

DOI: 10.1057/9781137370884

**APPENDIX A**   *Continued*

| | |
|---|---|
| *App2You, Inc.* | In 2010, NSF awarded $471,495 to App2You, Inc., a California-based company for a project titled, "Do-It-Yourself Database-Driven Web Applications from High Level Specifications." This project will enable non-programmers to rapidly create and evolve fully custom-hosted forms-driven workflow applications where users with different roles and rights interact. Such a platform will have a broad impact on organizations of all sizes by empowering nonprogrammer business-process owners to quickly and easily deploy applications that capture the business processes of their organizations. The platform has the maximum impact on enabling externally facing customer relationship management (CRM) for small and medium businesses (SMBs), which use the applications to facilitate and streamline interactions with customers and partners, achieve lower process-management and customer/partner servicing costs, increase customer/partner satisfaction and grow revenues. |

*Source*: Websites of the funding agencies. Also see Link and Scott (2012a, pp. 38–40).

**APPENDIX B**   *Examples of SBIR projects funded by the Department of Defense and used to evaluate the program*

| Funded company | Project description |
|---|---|
| *Materials Technology Corporation* | Materials Technology Corporation is a Connecticut-based company founded in 1986. Its SBIR Phase II project was titled "Life Prediction of Aging Aircraft Wiring Systems." The technology allows safe, accurate, and efficient diagnostic tests of the wiring in airplanes to ensure that the wiring is defect free. With the current technology, the inspector opens a panel door and examines bundles of wires with the naked eye. If the 12- to 18-inch section of wire that can be seen looks okay, then the entire wire is judged by the inspector to be safe. In some cases, the inspector may use a mirror to try to look at the back side of the wires, but because of visibility and space limitations it is rare that the back side is inspected well. The wires themselves are rarely a problem; instead, the insulation on the wires is what degrades, becoming brittle with age and cracking. The plasticizer vaporizes and, over time, the insulation degrades, becomes brittle, and begins to fall apart thus exposing bare wire. If two wires are exposed, a short circuit is possible. |

*Continued*

DOI: 10.1057/9781137370884

APPENDIX B    *Continued*

The new technology developed by Materials Technology Corporation is the first approach to inspecting for damaged insulation of wiring that allows viewing of all sides of the wiring and does not risk damaging the wires as typically occurs if the wires are bent or disturbed in trying to examine their back side. The technology uses embedded optical sensors in a device that can be put around the bundle of wires and used to achieve a 360-degree view of the wires. The information gathered by the handheld device is signaled to a computer that pinpoints and displays precisely where on the 360-degree surface a crack is located. New optical imaging technology is used to achieve this inspection ability. With the press of a button the image can be recorded and the data transported for use at other sites. The company expected that the system will allow the entre wiring history of the aircraft to be stored on a zip drive that will be carried in the aircraft. Planes will not have to return to a home base or home service area to be inspected and repaired. Historical data, supplemented with a visible image, will allow the inspector to see what the wiring looked like at the last inspection and to calculate the progression of changes.

In addition to examining aircraft wires and cables, the technology can be used to examine the connections and to detect corrosion more generally in aircraft or other objects.

There are many applications beyond those for the Department of Defense and commercial aircraft. The optical scanning procedure is expected to be relevant for dealing with vision problems caused by macular degeneration. And, of course, what is good for aircraft inspection is also good for inspecting bridges and other infrastructure.

*MicroCoating Technologies*    MicroCoating Technologies is a Georgia-based company founded in 1993. Its SBIR Phase II project was titled "Non-Chromate Combustion Chemical Vapor Deposition (CCVD) Coating for Naval Engine Components."

Hexavalent chrome is widely used in the Navy as well as in industry. However, it is a known carcinogen, and thus its use creates a toxic waste problem. The U.S. Environmental Protection Agency (EPA) knows of the problems associated with hexavalent chrome, but it has not yet mandated that it cease being used because no replacement is yet available (a common EPA practice). Congress has given DoD an internal directive to find a replacement material, and so, MicroCoating Technologies is developing such a material. The material is based on a thin-film oxide that can be applied to metal during a CCVD process. During that process, the thin film is sprayed on metal with a flame, and the residual gas contains a replacement molecular coating that performs like hexavalent chrome but has more environmentally friendly properties.[1]

*Continued*

DOI: 10.1057/9781137370884

**APPENDIX B**    *Continued*

| | |
|---|---|
| *Brock-Rogers Surgical* | Brock-Rogers Surgical is a Massachusetts-based company founded in 1995. Its SBIR Phase II project was titled "Development of a Force-Reflecting Laparoscopic Telemanipulator." |

The technology developed in the project merges technologies from electronics, mechanics, computer networking, and software to create a tele-robot to be used for surgery. The technology allows the surgeon to feel as if he or she were one inch tall and inside the patient. DoD is interested in such computer-augmented remote connections to allow medical personnel to operate on the front lines from remote locations. Beyond the military applications, such technology will change the face of surgery. A deep infrastructure technology is being created—a sophisticated electronic, mechanical, software-networked machine. In that sense, the technology is an enabling one with wide applications outside of medicine. The robot no longer needs to "see"—recognition and reception problems are handled by the human controlling the process.

*Summitec Corporation*    Summitec Corporation is a Tennessee-based company founded in 1987. Its SBIR Phase II project was titled "Very-Low-Bit-Rate-Error-Resilient Video Communication."

The lack of available bandwidth is the technical constraint on video imaging, especially wireless video imaging. With limited bandwidth, transmission of pictures is difficult and slow, and video is nearly impossible. Summitec is developing a compression-like software that will select only the important pieces of information to transmit over a narrow bandwidth so that video images will be clear. As the technical monitor explained, this software is like getting 10 pounds of potatoes into a 5 pound bag. The primary use of the software is in surveillance. Video information can be transmitted to planes to assist them in locational bombing.[2]

*Foster-Miller, Inc.*    Foster-Miller is a Massachusetts-based company founded in 1956. Its SBIR Phase II project was titled "Tunable Sting Net."

The technology developed in the project is the latest in a line of "NETS"—nonlethal entanglement technology systems—developed as SBIR projects by Foster-Miller in response to DoD's interest in funding research about capture mechanics. The nets developed by Foster-Miller are compact, light-weight, far-ranging, fast, and they can be fired from conventional weapons. The "Sting Net" delivers a remotely controlled electric charge for use with especially aggressive targets and is anticipated to have military applications. Less physically active versions range from nets that simply entangle to nets using pepper irritant powder to subdue more dangerous targets. The less harsh nets will have use in nonmilitary police operations.[3]

*Continued*

DOI: 10.1057/9781137370884

**APPENDIX B**   *Continued*

| | |
|---|---|
| *Matis, Inc.* | Matis, Inc. is a Georgia-based company founded in 1990. Its SBIR Phase II project was titled "A Novel Computational System for Real-Time Analysis and Prediction of Antenna-to-Aircraft and Antenna-to-Antenna Interactions."<br>There is a major problem with communication systems in general, and with antenna systems in particular. If antennas have no obstructions, then signals are transmitted and received clearly. However, such an environment rarely exists. On aircraft and ships, there often are obstructions of one form or another. These obstructions could be communications hardware or parts of the vehicle on which the communications are mounted. It is therefore critical to the quality of the communication system that the antennas be in an optimal position to minimize interference. Matis is developing software to simulate the antenna's environment and to measure the communication quality of alternative antenna placements. Given simulated information on alternative placements, it is the responsibility of engineers to trade off communication efficiency with engineering feasibility. The technology to develop this software comes from previous research projects.[4] |
| *QSource, Inc.* | QSource, Inc. is a Connecticut-based company founded in 1982. Its SBIR Phase II project was titled "Multiple Rectangular Discharge $CO_2$ Laser."<br>The laser technology developed generates high power and efficiency and has specialized military uses. There are also nonmilitary commercial applications with large market potential. QSource's laser features higher power, smaller size, and an advantage in cost. $CO_2$ lasers are used in laser radar to bounce a pulse off an object, with the high sensitivity allowing detailed information to be obtained about a tank or an aircraft many miles away. The laser system along with a DC battery source can be built in the size of a small suitcase. The $CO_2$ laser has very high efficiency, transmitting substantial distances with very little power loss; it is compact, uses a simple gas, and is very efficient.<br>The technology is dual use. The basic transmitter unit in the laser radar has applications for heating, cutting, and trimming, for example, in conjunction with one of the lasers used in eye surgery that was developed initially in another DoD-SBIR project trying to track objects at great distance. The laser is inherently sterile, and so, it is ideal for cutting tissue. It can be used for cutting teeth and as a mechanical drill. It is more expensive than a drill, but it eliminates the risk of transmitting hepatitis or other viruses. A laser dental system has a detachable head in the optical system that delivers the laser and is easy to clean. The surgery is painless; there is no need for anesthesia. The medical therapeutic uses include the dental applications, skin resurfacing, and microsurgery in the ear. Further markets have been identified for sealed $CO_2$ lasers in materials processing and various research applications. |

*Continued*

DOI: 10.1057/9781137370884

There are a large number of $CO_2$ lasers available and, over the last decade, they have become more functional. The cost of producing them in terms of dollars per watt is not great, but more than half of that cost is in the basic power source needed to energize the laser (i.e., powering the basic laser itself, not the entire system). The big advance provided by QSource technology is to reduce the cost of the power supply. Some of the older technology can achieve the same level of efficiency as the new QSource rectangular discharge laser, but those technologies result in products that are very big and not very sturdy.

**CG2, Inc.**    CG2, Inc. is an Alabama-based company founded in 1995. Its SBIR Phase II project was titled "Virtual Reality Scene Generalization by Means of Open Standards."

To test a missile, it has to be developed, tested under controlled conditions, and then fired. The model must be fired a significant number of times to verify its capabilities. The cost for each firing is between $10 million and $15 million. CG2 is investigating a lower-cost process for verifying the capabilities of a missile under development. The software that is being developed is designed to run a hardware-in-loop process. After a missile is launched once, all of the information from that launch is stored in a simulation computer. The simulation computer is then connected to the circuitry of a new missile, and to an image scene generator. Then the image scene generator is connected to the missile, completing the loop. The loop first repeats for the new missile the flight of the tested missile. Then, there is what is called a validated simulation. Once the simulation is validated, the missile can be tested in various environments that are created by the image scene generator. For example, the image scene generator can tell the missile that it is seeing various things (e.g., a mountain) and it will measure how the missile reacts. The missile's reaction is stored in the simulation computer. Once completed, this technology can save the DoD billions of dollars per year in unneeded missile firings.[5]

**Mide Technology Corp.**    Mide Technology Corp. is a Massachusetts-based company founded in 1989. Its SBIR Phase II project was titled "Development of Distributed Area Averaging Sensor."

The technology developed in the project eliminates harmful vibrations in structures by use of active materials that respond to stimuli; for example, if voltage is applied, the active material expands or contracts. The vibrations of structures have several natural frequencies, and the technology developed by Mide Technology Corporation uses shaped sensors to filter out noise, focusing on a desired frequency to eliminate the associated vibrations. The area averaging sensor simplifies a higher-dimension multi-input/multi-output information

*Continued*

DOI: 10.1057/9781137370884

**APPENDIX B**    *Continued*

problem to a lower-dimension control system that characterizes
more simply the necessary information about the natural frequencies
causing vibrations, despite a complex set of underlying information.
The frequencies that really transmit the noise through the structure
of interest can be isolated using a control system with active fiber
composite actuators; the smart material is used to simplify the control
problem and, ultimately, to allow the elimination of the vibrations
from the structure.

The immediate application of the technology is to protect launch
satellites from damage from structural vibrations. Alternatively, one
could protect the launch satellite with blankets—thin ones to protect
against high-frequency noise, and thick ones to protect against
lower-frequency noise. The Mide technology is the active way of
dealing with the problem. Commercial potential extends beyond the
protection from vibration of components in space launch vehicles.
The commercial potential comes from using area average sensors
with flexible circuitry, and Mide has four commercial products using
that technology. The products range from generic technology such as
sensors on a flexible circuitry for signal conditioning, a high-voltage
amplifier to drive active fiber composites, and sensors connected in
various ways on a small matrix board, to a specific application that
uses sensors on the shaft of a golf club to detect club head speed and
provide feedback. The generic applications range from military uses
such as protecting the launch of a spacecraft or quieting torpedoes in
a submarine to nonmilitary commercial uses such as vibration control
for the blades of a gas turbine or in air-conditioning ducts. Anything
that vibrates and has a dynamics problem with the vibration and noise
can potentially benefit from the technology.

*Bevilacqua*
*Research*
*Corporation*

Bevilacqua Research Corporation is an Alabama-based company
founded in 1992. Its SBIR Phase II project was titled "A Dialectic
Approach to Intelligence Data Fusion for Threat Identification."

The goal of this project is to produce a software architecture that will
make computers think more like people think. DoD has a strong
desire to be able to do intelligent programming. It has attempted
this in the past through what was called "role-based expert systems."
That technology worked fine in a FORTRAN world of "if this,
then that." However, the needs of DoD are more complex, and
alternative technology is needed. The software being developed will
take systematic concepts and translate them into numbers so that
the computer can process them. For example, when people think of
a concept, they do so in terms of a vector of characteristics of the
concept. However, if two concepts are combined, then the vector of
characteristics of the combined concepts is not necessarily a linear
combination of the individual concept vectors. Bevilacqua calls this
architecture a "cognitive reasoning engine."[6]

*Source:* Link (2000, pp. 204–210) and Scott (2000b, pp. 106–114).

DOI: 10.1057/9781137370884

# Notes

1   Based on discussions with the management of the company, this project
    would not have occurred in the absence of SBIR funding. In fact, the
    company would not be in business. According to management, venture
    capitalists were simply not interested in materials science.

2   The company reported that outside investors were very difficult to locate
    because the commercial return to the technology was not expected to occur
    quickly. Investors saw the long-time to market as a problem.

3   The Sting Net project fits with Foster-Miller's highly successful corporate
    strategy of inventing and licensing patented technologies, and spinning
    off subsidiary companies to manufacture and market the innovations.
    Numerous SBIR projects have contributed to that strategy, although the
    company gets only about 20 to 25 percent of its revenues from the SBIR
    awards.

4   Management reported that in the absence of SBIR funding, Matis likely
    would have taken on this project on a limited scale. Although the capital and
    labor costs to undertake the research were extraordinarily high, Matis had
    previous investment relationships with companies and could have acquired
    partial funding.

5   Because of the high capital costs for this research and the lack of available
    funding sources, management reports that this research would not have been
    undertaken in the absence of the SBIR award. Outside investors would not
    have been interested because the market is so small, and the technology can
    be imitated quickly.

6   The company reported that it would not have undertaken the development
    of the new concept without the SBIR funding for two reasons. First, it did
    not have access to sufficient funding because the commercial applications
    of the technology would not have been readily understood by investors.
    Second, the architecture can be imitated quickly once commercialized.

DOI: 10.1057/9781137370884

# References

Archibald, Robert B. and David H. Finifter (2000). "Evaluation of the Department of Defense Small Business Innovation Research Program and Fast Track Initiative: A Balanced Approach," in *The Small Business Innovation Research Program: An Assessment of the Department of Defense Fast Track Initiative*, edited by C.W. Wessner, Washington, DC: National Academy Press, pp. 211–250.

▶ Arrow, Kenneth J. (1962). "Economic Welfare and the Allocation of Resources for Invention," in *The Rate and Direction of Inventive Activity: Economic and Social Factors*, edited by R.R. Nelson, Princeton, NJ: Princeton University Press, pp. 609–626.

Audretsch, David B., Albert N. Link, and John T. Scott (2002). "Public/Private Technology Partnerships: Evaluating SBIR-Supported Research," *Research Policy* 31: 145–158.

Audretsch, David B. and A. Roy Thurik (2001). "What's New about the New Economy? Sources of Growth in the Managed and Entrepreneurial Economies," *Industrial and Corporate Change* 10: 267–315.

Audretsch, David B. and A. Roy Thurik (2004). "A Model of the Entrepreneurial Economy," *International Journal of Entrepreneurship Education* 2: 143–166.

Birch, David L. (1979). *The Job Generation Process*, Cambridge, MA: MIT Program on Neighborhood and Regional Change.

Birch, David L. (1981). "Who Creates Jobs?" *Public Interest* 65: 3–14.

DOI: 10.1057/9781137370884

Birch, David L. (1987). *Job Creation in America: How Our Smallest Companies Put the Most People to Work*, New York: Free Press.

Branscomb, Lewis M. and Philip E. Auerswald (2002). *Between Invention and Innovation: An Analysis of Funding for Early-Stage Technology Development*, Washington, DC: U.S. Department of Commerce.

Cantillon, Richard (1931). *Essai sur la Nature du commerce en General*, edited by H. Higgs. London: Palgrave Macmillan.

Carlsson, Bo (1992). "The Rise of Small Business: Causes and Consequences," in *Singular Europe: Economy and Polity of the European Community after 1992*, edited by W. J. Adams, Ann Arbor, MI: University of Michigan Press, pp. 145–169.

Ehlers, Vernon (2000). Unpublished lecture to the conference on basic research in service of national objectives. November 28, as referenced in Branscomb and Auerswald (2002).

Hall, Bronwyn H., Albert N. Link, and John T. Scott (2000). "Universities as Research Partners," NBER Working Paper 7643.

Hall, Bronwyn H., Albert N. Link, and John T. Scott (2003). "Universities as Research Partners," *Review of Economics and Statistics* 85: 485–491.

Hébert, Robert F. and Albert N. Link (1988). *The Entrepreneur: Mainstream Views and Radical Critiques*, New York: Praeger.

Hébert, Robert F. and Albert N. Link (2006). "Historical Perspectives on the Entrepreneur," *Foundations and Trends in Entrepreneurship* 2: 261–408.

Hébert, Robert F. and Albert N. Link (2009). *A History of Entrepreneurship*, London: Routledge.

Lerner, Josh (1999). "The Government as Venture Capitalist: The Long-Run Impact of the SBIR Program," *The Journal of Business* 72: 285–318.

Lerner, Josh, and Colin Kegler (2000). "Evaluating the Small Business Innovation Research Program: A Literature Review," in *The Small Business Innovation Research Program: An Assessment of the Department of Defense Fast Track Initiative*, edited by Charles W. Wessner, Washington, DC: National Academy Press, pp. 307–324.

Link, Albert N. (2000). "An Assessment of the Small Business Innovation Research Fast Track Program in the Southeastern States," in *The Small Business Innovation Research Program: An Assessment of the Department of Defense Fast Track Initiative*, edited by C.W. Wessner, Washington, DC: National Academy Press, pp. 194–210.

DOI: 10.1057/9781137370884

Link, Albert N. (2011). "Small Business Innovation Research Program," Testimony before the Committee on Small Business, Subcommittee on Healthcare and Technology, United States House of Representatives, under *The Creating Jobs through Small Business Innovation Act of 2011*, April 7, 2011.

Link, Albert N. and Jamie R. Link (2009). *Government as Entrepreneur*, New York: Oxford University Press.

Link, Albert N. and John T. Scott (2000). "Estimates of the Social Returns to Small Business Innovation Research Projects," in *The Small Business Innovation Research Program: An Assessment of the Department of Defense Fast Track Initiative*, edited by C.W. Wessner, Washington, DC: National Academy Press, pp. 275–290.

Link, Albert N. and John T. Scott (2009). "Private Investor Participation and Commercialization Rates for Government-Sponsored Research and Development: Would a Prediction Market Improve the Performance of the SBIR Programme?" *Economica* 76: 264–281.

Link, Albert N. and John T. Scott (2010). "Government as Entrepreneur: Evaluating the Commercialization Success of SBIR Projects," *Research Policy* 39: 589–601.

Link, Albert N. and John T. Scott (2011). *Public Goods, Public Gains: Calculating the Social Benefits of Public R&D*, New York: Oxford University Press.

Link, Albert N. and John T. Scott (2012a). *Employment Growth from Public Support of Innovation in Small Firms*, Kalamazoo, MI: W.E. Upjohn Institute for Employment Research.

Link, Albert N. and John T. Scott (2012b). "Employment Growth from Public Support of Innovation in Small Firms," *Economics of Innovation and New Technology* 21: 655–678.

Link, Albert N. and John T. Scott (2012c). "Employment Growth from the Small Business Innovation Research Program," *Small Business Economics* 39: 265–287.

Link, Albert N. and John T. Scott (2012d). "The Exploitation of Publicly Funded Technology," *Journal of Technology Transfer* 37: 375–383.

Link, Albert N. and John T. Scott (2012e). "The Small Business Innovation Research Program," *Issues in Science and Technology*, summer: 89–92.

Link, Albert N. and John T. Scott (2012f). "On the Social Value of Quality: An Economic Evaluation of the Baldrige Performance Excellence Program," *Science and Public Policy* 39: 680–689.

DOI: 10.1057/9781137370884

Link, Albert N. and John T. Scott (forthcoming). "Public R&D Subsidies, Outside Private Support, and Employment Growth," *Economics of Innovation and New Technology*.

Martin, Stephen and John T. Scott (2000). "The Nature of Innovation Market Failure and the Design of Public Support for Private Innovation," *Research Policy* 29: 437–477.

Nelson, R. R. (1982). "Government Stimulus of Technological Progress: Lessons from American History," in *Government and Technical Progress*, edited by R. R. Nelson, New York: Pergamon, pp. 451–482.

Schacht, Wendy H. (2012). "Small Business Innovation Research (SBIR) Program," Congressional Research Service Report to Congress, Washington, DC: Congressional Research Service.

Schultz, Theodore W. (1980). "Investment in Entrepreneurial Ability," *Scandinavian Journal of Economics* 82: 437–448.

Schumpeter, Joseph A. (1928). "The Instability of Capitalism," *Economic Journal* 38: 361–386.

Scott, John T. (2000a). "The Directions for Technological Change: Alternative Economic Majorities and Opportunity Costs," *Review of Industrial Organization* 17: 1–16.

Scott, John T. (2000b). "An Assessment of the Small Business Innovation Research Program in New England: Fast Track Compared with Non-Fast Track Projects," in *The Small Business Innovation Research Program: An Assessment of the Department of Defense Fast Track Initiative*, edited by C.W. Wessner, Washington, DC: National Academy Press, pp. 104–140.

Tibbetts, Ronald (1999). "The Small Business Innovation Research Program and NSF SBIR Commercialization Results," in *SBIR—The Small Business Innovation Research Program Challenges and Opportunities*, edited by C.W. Wessner, Washington, DC: National Academy Press, pp. 129–167.

U.S. Senate (2008). *SBIR/STTR Reauthorization Act of 2008*, Senate Report 100–447, Washington, DC: U.S. Government Printing Office.

Wessner, Charles W. (2000). *The Small Business Innovation Research Program: An Assessment of the Department of Defense Fast Track Initiative*, Washington, DC: National Academy Press.

Wessner, Charles W. (2008). *An Assessment of the SBIR Program*, Washington, DC: National Academy Press.

White House Blog (2013a). "A Whole-of-Government Commitment to Inclusive Entrepreneurial Growth," <http://www.whitehouse.

DOI: 10.1057/9781137370884

gov/blog/2013/01/07/whole-government-commitment-inclusive-entrepreneurial-growth>.

White House Blog (2013b). "Startup America," <http://www.whitehouse.gov/economy/business/startup-america>.

Wolfers, Justin and Eric Zitzewitz (2004). "Prediction Markets," *Journal of Economic Perspectives*, 18: 107–126.

Wolfers, Justin and Eric Zitzewitz (2006). "Interpreting Prediction Market Prices as Probabilities," NBER Working Paper No. 12083.

Zeckhauser, Richard (1996). "The Challenge of Contracting for Technological Information," *Proceedings of the National Academy of Science* 93: 12743–12748.

DOI: 10.1057/9781137370884

# Index

DOI: 10.1057/9781137370884

GPSR Compliance
The European Union's (EU) General Product Safety Regulation (GPSR) is a set
of rules that requires consumer products to be safe and our obligations to
ensure this.

If you have any concerns about our products, you can contact us on

ProductSafety@springernature.com

In case Publisher is established outside the EU, the EU authorized
representative is:

Springer Nature Customer Service Center GmbH
Europaplatz 3
69115 Heidelberg, Germany